The Bite Marked Heart

By

Alwy M. Jones

Buy Me Coffee

Fait Accompli

Rising Down

"You're not to be so blind with patriotism that you can't face reality. Wrong is wrong, no matter who does it or says it."

El-Hajj Malik El-Shabazz

PREFACE

In an era where the rhetoric of human rights and protection often masks the reality of state sanctioned violence, this book delves into a chilling paradox; the targeted killings of ordinary citizens, community leaders, religious figures, and innocent civilians by governments that claim to uphold human rights. The historical and contemporary landscape is rife with examples where state actors justify their lethal actions under the guise of maintaining order and security. These governments employ narratives of safety to veil their transgressions against the very people they are sworn to protect.

The emotional toll of these killings is profound and far reaching. Each life lost ripples through families and communities, leaving behind a trail of grief, trauma, and dislocation. Imagine a child witnessing the murder of a parent, an experience that not only shatters their sense of safety but also plunges them into psychological distress. The stories of those affected are not mere statistics; they are poignant reminders of the human cost of state violence. Families are torn apart, communities are fractured, and societies become shadows of their former selves, haunted by loss and fear.

The purpose of this book is threefold; to raise awareness about these atrocities, to foster dialogue around the implications of such state actions, and to advocate for accountability in international law. By shedding light on these grave violations, we aim to challenge the narratives propagated by oppressive regimes that seek to normalize violence against their others. It is imperative that we confront these realities head-on, not only to honor those who have suffered but also to prevent future injustices. Within these pages, we will explore various dimensions of targeted killings through a structured examination of case studies and personal narratives.

Hind Rajab

On January 29th 2024, a tragic incident unfolded in Gaza that captured international attention, resulting in the death of six year old Hind Rajab. The young girl was killed during an Israeli military operation, with subsequent investigations revealing that her little body bore multiple bullet wounds with a total of 335 bullets fired at the car in which she and her relatives occupied. This incident has sparked outrage and calls for accountability amid the ongoing Israeli-Palestinian conflict.

The Israeli-Palestinian conflict has been marked by decades of violence, significantly impacting civilians, particularly children. According to reports, over 41,000 Palestinian children have died since the escalation of hostilities in October 2023. The conflict has resulted in severe humanitarian crises, with many families displaced and essential services disrupted. The United Nations estimates that nearly half of Gaza's population are children, underscoring the vulnerability of this demographic amidst ongoing violence.

Hind Rajab's death occurred as she and her family attempted to flee from escalating violence in northern Gaza. On the day of the incident, they were trapped in their vehicle when it came under fire from an Israeli tank. Eyewitness accounts detail a harrowing scene where Hind made desperate calls to paramedics and her mother, pleading for help as she remained alive among the bodies of her deceased relatives.

Investigations by Forensic Architecture and other organizations concluded that an Israeli tank fired upon their car from a distance of just 13 to 23 meters. The Israeli Defense Forces (IDF) initially denied responsibility for the attack, claiming no troops were present in the area. However, satellite imagery and forensic analysis contradicted this assertion, showing that Israeli tanks were indeed nearby and had clear visibility of the car's occupants.

The autopsy findings revealed that Hind Rajab's body contained multiple bullet wounds, raising serious concerns about military conduct and rules of engagement. Such a high number of bullets suggests excessive force was used against a civilian vehicle clearly occupied by children. This incident parallels other documented cases where civilians have been disproportionately affected by military actions in Gaza, highlighting a troubling pattern of violence against non-combatants.

The local and international reactions to Hind's death were swift and intense. Human rights organizations condemned the attack as a violation of international law, calling for accountability from the Israeli government. Protests erupted globally as activists rallied for justice for Hind Rajab and other victims of similar violence. The media coverage varied significantly, with some outlets criticized for failing to attribute responsibility directly to Israeli forces.

Dr. Adnan Al-Bursh

Dr. Adnan Al-Bursh, a prominent Palestinian orthopedic surgeon and the head of orthopedics at Al-Shifa Hospital in Gaza, became a symbol of resilience amidst the ongoing conflict in the region. His tragic death in an Israeli prison after four months of detention raises critical questions about human rights violations and the treatment of medical professionals in conflict zones.

Dr. Adnan Al-Bursh was born in Gaza and pursued his medical education with a focus on orthopedic surgery, eventually becoming one of the most respected surgeons in the region. He was known for his dedication to patient care and his expertise in treating traumatic injuries, particularly those resulting from the ongoing violence in Gaza. Over the years, he earned a reputation not only as a skilled surgeon but also as a compassionate caregiver who documented the struggles faced by his patients during times of war. As the head of orthopedics at Al-Shifa Hospital, Gaza's largest medical facility, Dr. Al-Bursh played a crucial role in providing emergency care during periods of intense conflict. His efforts were particularly notable during escalations in violence when he worked tirelessly to treat injured civilians, often under dire conditions. Reports indicate that he frequently operated long hours without adequate supplies or rest, showcasing his commitment to saving lives despite overwhelming challenges. Dr. Al-Bursh became well known for his ability to perform complex surgeries under pressure, often sharing harrowing accounts of his experiences through social media and interviews, which highlighted the humanitarian crisis unfolding around him. His documentation included images and videos that captured both the physical toll on patients and the emotional strain on medical staff.

In December 2023, amidst escalating military operations in Gaza, Dr. Al-Bursh was detained by Israeli forces while providing care at Al-Awada Hospital. He was one of several medical personnel apprehended during military incursions into areas heavily impacted by conflict. Following his arrest, reports emerged detailing severe mistreatment during his detention. Witnesses from within Israeli prisons later recounted that Dr. Al-Bursh had been subjected to brutal torture, including beatings and psychological abuse. A fellow inmate described finding him in a deplorable state upon arrival at Ofer Prison, indicating that he had been assaulted and left to suffer without medical attention. His death on April 19th 2024, was officially acknowledged by Israeli authorities but surrounded by allegations of torture leading to his demise.

According to a deposition provided to HaMoked, an Israeli human rights organization, by a prisoner who knew Al-Bursh, he was injured upon his arrival at Ofer in mid-April and was "naked in the lower part of his body". The deposition said that guards threw him down in the yard and left him there, unable to stand up, and that he died shortly after being helped to a room by prisoners. The Israel Prison Service denied these events.

Al-Bursh's body was kept in Israeli custody, and the fate of the other detained medical workers remains uncertain. In May 2024, the family of Al-Bursh had a lawyer from The Hague look into his death and help facilitate the return of his body. On 15th May, Al-Bursh's wife and Physicians for Human Rights Israel submitted a request for an investigation and autopsy to the Jerusalem Magistrate Court.

The circumstances surrounding Dr. Al-Bursh's death have sparked outrage among human rights organizations and advocacy groups who view his treatment as part of a broader pattern of systematic abuse against Palestinian healthcare workers. Palestinian prisoner associations have condemned his death as an "assassination," asserting it reflects an intentional campaign against medical professionals operating in Gaza.

International responses have included calls for investigations into alleged human rights violations committed by Israeli forces against detainees. Human Rights Watch has documented widespread abuse within Israeli detention facilities, emphasizing that such mistreatment is not isolated but part of a larger issue affecting many Palestinians detained under similar circumstances.

Reham Ishneiwra

Reham Ishneiwra was a distinguished Palestinian academic and a dedicated scholar in the field of biotechnology. As a lecturer in the Department of Biotechnology at Al-Azhar University in Gaza, she made significant contributions to her field, focusing on research that aimed to address local health challenges through biotechnological innovations. Ishneiwra's work was not only academically rigorous but also deeply rooted in the socio-political context of Palestine, where access to healthcare and scientific resources is often compromised due to ongoing conflict.

The historical and political context of Reham Ishneiwra's life and work is essential to understanding the implications of her death. The Israeli-Palestinian conflict has persisted for decades, characterized by territorial disputes, military confrontations, and significant humanitarian crises. Key events leading up to her death include the ongoing blockade of Gaza, repeated military incursions, and heightened tensions following the 2023 escalation of violence, which severely impacted daily life and academic activities in the region. The conflict has created an environment where academics face not only professional challenges but also personal risks. The systematic targeting of intellectuals and professionals during periods of unrest has been documented, contributing to a climate of fear that stifles innovation and critical thought.

Reham Ishneiwra was killed on March 15th 2024, during an Israeli military operation in Gaza City. Eyewitness accounts describe a chaotic scene as Israeli forces conducted airstrikes and ground operations targeting alleged militant positions in densely populated areas. Reports indicate that Ishneiwra was caught in crossfire while attempting to evacuate students from her university during a sudden escalation of violence. The incident drew immediate attention from local media and human rights organizations. Eyewitnesses recounted how she bravely led her students to safety when she was struck by shrapnel from an explosion nearby. Official statements from Al-Azhar University condemned her death as a tragic loss for Palestinian academia and called for an independent investigation into the circumstances surrounding her killing.

Credible organizations such as Human Rights Watch and Amnesty International issued statements highlighting the need for accountability regarding civilian casualties during military operations in Gaza, emphasizing that such incidents often disproportionately affect women and children.

The academic community both locally and internationally reacted with shock and outrage following Ishneiwra's death. Colleagues at Al-Azhar University mourned the loss of a dedicated educator who inspired many students through her passion for science and commitment to social issues.

Sheikh Anwar Al-Awlaki

Sheikh Anwar Al-Awlaki was a prominent American-Yemeni cleric whose life and activities became emblematic of the complex intersections between religion, politics, and terrorism in the post 9/11 world. Born on April 22nd 1971, in Las Cruces, New Mexico, Al-Awlaki spent his formative years in Yemen before returning to the United States for higher education. He earned a Bachelor's degree in Civil Engineering from Colorado State University and later pursued a Master's degree in Educational Leadership at San Diego State University.

Anwar Al-Awlaki's troubles began in 2006 when he was detained by Yemeni authorities. His arrest was reportedly linked to his involvement in a local tribal dispute and allegations of connections to militant activities. Although he was never formally charged with any crime, Al-Awlaki spent 18 months in prison, where he endured significant hardships. During his detention, he was subjected to interrogations by both Yemeni officials and U.S. agents, including the FBI. Eyewitness accounts and interviews with Al-Awlaki after his release reveal that he faced psychological pressure and harsh treatment while imprisoned. He described being held in solitary confinement and experiencing limited access to family and legal representation. In interviews conducted post-release, Al-Awlaki recounted that the U.S. had requested his detention due to concerns about his sermons and potential influence on radicalization among Muslims.

Human rights organizations have documented instances of torture and ill treatment in Yemeni prisons, raising serious concerns about the legality and morality of such actions. Reports indicate that detainees often face physical abuse, psychological torture, and inadequate medical care while under custody.

Al-Awlaki's release from Yemeni custody occurred in 2007 after significant public outcry and advocacy from human rights groups who argued that his detention lacked legal justification. His exoneration was influenced by mounting evidence that he had not committed any crimes warranting imprisonment. Upon release, Al-Awlaki issued statements condemning his treatment in prison while also expressing a desire to return to public life. In the immediate aftermath of his release, Al-Awlaki reestablished himself as a prominent voice within Islamist circles. He began producing online lectures that attracted significant attention from individuals worldwide. He condemned U.S. foreign policy towards Muslims.

In July 2010, al-Awlaki's father, Nasser al-Awlaki, contacted the Center for Constitutional Rights and the American Civil Liberties Union to represent his son in a lawsuit that sought to remove Anwar from the targeted killing list. On August 30th 2010, the groups filed a "targeted killing" lawsuit, naming President Obama, CIA Director Leon Panetta, and Secretary of Defense Robert Gates as defendants. They sought an injunction preventing the targeted killing of al-Awlaki, and also sought to require the government to disclose the standards under which U.S. citizens may be "targeted for death".

On September 30th 2011, Anwar Al-Awlaki was killed in a U.S. drone strike in the Al Jawf Governorate of Yemen. The operation was carried out by the Joint Special Operations Command (JSOC) with the involvement of the CIA. This targeted killing marked a significant escalation in U.S. counterterrorism tactics, particularly concerning American citizens abroad. Reports indicate that Al-Awlaki was traveling with several associates when their convoy was struck by missiles fired from an unmanned aerial vehicle (UAV). Eyewitness accounts describe a scene of chaos following the strike, with local residents confirming that Al-Awlaki was among those killed.

Anwar al-Awlaki and Egyptian born Gihan Mohsen Baker had a son; Abdulrahman Anwar al-Awlaki, born August 26th 1995 in Denver, who was an American citizen. Abdulrahman al-Awlaki was killed on October 14th 2011, in Yemen at the age of 16 in an American drone strike. Nine other people were killed in the same CIA initiated attack, including a 17 year old cousin of Abdulrahman. According to his relatives, shortly before his father's death, Abdulrahman had left the family home in Sana'a and travelled to Shabwa in search of his father who was believed to be in that area (though he was actually hundreds of miles away at the time). Abdulrahman was sitting in an open air cafe in Shabwa when killed.

Human rights organizations expressed concern over the implications of targeted drone strikes on international law and human rights standards. The case prompted discussions about accountability for extrajudicial killings and the need for clearer guidelines governing such operations.

Omar Al-Mukhtar

Omar Al-Mukhtar, born in 1862 in Tobruk, Libya, emerged as a pivotal figure in the resistance against Italian colonization. His early life as a teacher of the Qur'an laid the foundation for his leadership qualities and commitment to his people's struggle for independence. As the leader of the Libyan resistance movement, Al-Mukhtar became a symbol of resilience and courage against colonial oppression, inspiring generations to fight for their rights and freedoms.

Omar Al-Mukhtar was born into a respected family of the Minfi tribe. After losing his father during a pilgrimage to Mecca, he was raised by his uncle in accordance with Islamic teachings. He pursued his education at the Jagbub Institute, where he studied various Islamic sciences, including jurisprudence and hadith. His dedication to education led him to become a teacher of the Qur'an, where he influenced many young Libyans and became involved with the Senussi Order, an Islamic revivalist movement that played a crucial role in resisting colonial powers in North Africa.

The historical context of Italian colonization began in 1911 when Italy invaded Libya, claiming it was liberating the territory from Ottoman rule. The Libyans initially resisted but faced brutal military campaigns. Following the rise of Benito Mussolini, Italian forces intensified their efforts to suppress the Libyan populace. Omar Al-Mukhtar's resistance began earnestly in the 1920s when he organized guerrilla warfare tactics against Italian troops. His leadership style was characterized by strategic ambushes and deep knowledge of the desert terrain, which he used to outmaneuver Italian forces. Key battles included those at Kufra and Uadi Bu Taga, where his forces engaged in fierce combat despite being outnumbered. His ability to inspire loyalty among his followers and unite various tribes under a common cause made him a formidable opponent.

On September 11th 1931, during a battle near Slonta, Omar Al-Mukhtar was wounded and captured by Libyan Savaris serving the Italian Army. His capture marked a significant turning point in the resistance movement. Following his capture, he was tried in a military court on September 15th 1931. Despite his eloquent defense and expressions of faith, he was sentenced to death. Al-Mukhtar was executed on September 16th 1931, at the age of 73 in Soluch concentration camp. His execution was intended by the Italians to serve as a warning to other potential resistors; however, it only solidified his status as a martyr for Libyan independence.

The immediate impact of Omar Al-Mukhtar's execution was profound; it galvanized further resistance against Italian rule. Despite Italian hopes that his death would quell dissent, his legacy continued to inspire Libyans in their struggle for independence. The brutal tactics employed by the Italians during their colonial rule only fueled resentment among the populace.

In subsequent years, Al-Mukhtar became an enduring symbol of resistance not only in Libya but across the Arab world. His life has been commemorated in literature and film, notably in "Lion of the Desert," which portrays his heroic struggle against colonial oppression. His legacy is honored through monuments and public memory as a testament to the fight against tyranny.

- Omar Al-Mukhtar's execution by hanging

el-Hajj Malik el-Shabazz

el-Hajj Malik el-Shabazz, widely known as Malcolm X, stands as a towering figure in American history, renowned for his revolutionary fervor and his commitment to human rights activism. Born Malcolm Little on May 19th 1925, he became a prominent voice for African American empowerment during the civil rights movement. His advocacy for Black self-determination and critique of systemic racism positioned him as a controversial yet essential figure in the struggle for racial equality. Malcolm X's enduring influence continues to resonate in contemporary movements for social justice and human rights.

Malcolm X was born in Omaha, Nebraska, to Earl and Louise Little. His father was a minister and an active supporter of Marcus Garvey's Universal Negro Improvement Association, which emphasized Black Nationalism. The family faced severe racial hostility, including threats from white supremacist groups like the Ku Klux Klan. In 1931, following the mysterious death of his father, believed to be a murder by white supremacists, his mother suffered a mental breakdown, leading to the children being placed in foster care. Malcolm experienced significant racism throughout his childhood, which deeply influenced his worldview. He excelled academically but dropped out of school at age 15 after being discouraged from pursuing his dream of becoming a lawyer by a teacher who deemed it unrealistic for a Black child.

Subsequently, he moved to Boston to live with his half-sister and became involved in criminal activities, including drug dealing and burglary. In 1946, he was arrested and sentenced to ten years in prison. While incarcerated, Malcolm X encountered the teachings of the Nation of Islam (NOI) through correspondence with his siblings who were already members. He converted to Islam and adopted the surname "X" to symbolize his lost African heritage. Upon his release in 1952, he quickly rose within the ranks of the NOI due to his charisma and oratory skills. As a minister, Malcolm X became one of the most influential spokespeople for the Nation of Islam. He delivered powerful speeches advocating for Black empowerment and criticized the mainstream civil rights movement's emphasis on non-violence and integration. His rhetoric often included calls for self-defense "by any means necessary," which resonated with many African Americans frustrated by systemic oppression. Under his leadership, the NOI experienced significant growth in membership and visibility. By the early 1960s, Malcolm X began to experience ideological rifts with the Nation of Islam's leadership, particularly Elijah Muhammad. Disillusioned by Muhammad's personal conduct and the organization's refusal to engage with broader civil rights efforts, Malcolm sought new directions for his activism.

In 1964, he made a transformative pilgrimage to Mecca (Hajj), where he encountered Muslims of all races united in faith. This experience profoundly changed his perspective on race relations; he began to embrace a more inclusive view that emphasized universal brotherhood among all people. Upon returning to America, he publicly renounced the Nation of Islam and adopted the name el-Hajj Malik el-Shabazz. Following his break from the NOI, Malcolm X founded several organizations aimed at promoting human rights and addressing systemic racism. He established the Organization of Afro-American Unity (OAAU) in 1964, modeled after the Organization of African Unity. The OAAU sought to unite African Americans in their struggle for rights and dignity while promoting Pan-African solidarity. Malcolm X's speeches during this period reflected his evolving views on race and justice. He advocated for political engagement among African Americans and called for international support against colonialism and imperialism affecting people of African descent globally. His famous speech "The Ballot or the Bullet" articulated these ideas powerfully, emphasizing that African Americans must assert their rights through political action or self-defense if necessary.

On February 21st 1965, Malcolm X was assassinated at the Audubon Ballroom in Manhattan while preparing to address a meeting of the OAAU. Just days prior, he had expressed concerns about threats against him from former allies within the Nation of Islam. During his speech that day, gunmen affiliated with the NOI opened fire; Malcolm was shot multiple times and pronounced dead shortly thereafter.

Steve Bantu Biko

Steve Bantu Biko emerged as one of the most significant anti-apartheid activists in South Africa during the late 20th century. As a leader of the Black Consciousness Movement (BCM), Biko's activism was pivotal in fostering a sense of pride and self-worth among black South Africans, challenging the dehumanizing effects of apartheid. His contributions not only galvanized a generation but also laid the groundwork for future resistance against the oppressive regime. Tragically, Biko's life was cut short when he died in police custody in 1977, an event that sparked international outrage and further fueled the anti-apartheid movement.

Steve Biko was born on December 18th 1946, in King William's Town, Eastern Cape, South Africa. He was the third of four children in a middle class family; his father was a police officer, and his mother was a homemaker. Biko's early life was marked by the harsh realities of apartheid, which deeply influenced his worldview. Biko attended local schools and later enrolled at the University of Natal Medical School in 1966. It was during his university years that he became actively involved in student politics. He co-founded the South African Students' Organization (SASO) in 1968, which aimed to provide a platform for black students to voice their grievances against the apartheid system. SASO became instrumental in mobilizing student activism and promoting black consciousness among youth.

The Black Consciousness Movement, spearheaded by Biko, sought to empower black South Africans by fostering a sense of identity and pride. The movement emphasized psychological liberation as a prerequisite for political freedom, arguing that internalized racism must be addressed before meaningful resistance could occur. Biko articulated that "the most potent weapon in the hands of the oppressor is the mind of the oppressed," highlighting the need for mental emancipation alongside physical liberation. The BCM sought to instill pride through slogans like "Black is Beautiful," encouraging black individuals to reject notions of inferiority imposed by a racist society. Key initiatives led by Biko included community development programs and educational campaigns aimed at uplifting black communities. The movement also organized protests and demonstrations against apartheid policies, significantly contributing to the broader anti-apartheid struggle.

On August 18th 1977, Steve Biko was arrested under Section 83 of the Terrorism Act, which allowed for detention without trial. His arrest marked the beginning of a brutal period of torture at the hands of South African security forces. While in custody, Biko endured severe beatings and psychological torment. Reports indicate that he was chained to a metal window for an entire day without food or water. Despite his deteriorating condition, authorities refused to provide adequate medical care. The treatment he received exemplified the extreme measures employed by the apartheid regime to suppress dissenting voices. Biko's resilience during this time further galvanized public support for his cause.

On September 11th 1977, after enduring weeks of torture, Steve Biko was found dead in police custody. In an attempt to cover up their actions, authorities claimed he had died from a hunger strike; however, autopsy reports revealed extensive injuries consistent with torture. Biko's death ignited widespread outrage both domestically and internationally. The brutality surrounding his demise highlighted the violent nature of apartheid rule and drew global attention to the plight of black South Africans. Prominent figures such as journalist Donald Woods worked tirelessly to expose the truth behind Biko's death, further amplifying calls for justice.

Huey P. Newton

Huey P. Newton emerged as a transformative revolutionary figure during a critical period of racial tension and social upheaval in American history. As a co-founder of the Black Panther Party, Newton embodied a radical approach to civil rights that challenged systemic racism through direct action, community organizing, and a revolutionary political ideology. His leadership represented a pivotal moment in African American political activism, moving beyond traditional civil rights strategies to advocate for comprehensive social transformation. The Black Panther Party's ten point manifesto, authored by Newton and Bobby Seale, articulated a comprehensive vision of Black empowerment that went far beyond mere legal equality. It demanded fundamental societal restructuring, addressing issues of economic justice, education, housing, and self-determination for African American communities.

Born on February 17th 1942, in Oak Grove, Louisiana, Huey Percy Newton grew up in Oakland, California, experiencing firsthand the complex racial dynamics of post-World War II urban America. The son of Walter and Armelia Newton, both sharecroppers who migrated from the rural South, Huey was deeply influenced by the Great Migration's transformative social experiences. Newton's early education was marked by significant challenges. Despite initial academic struggles and being labeled as functionally illiterate, he demonstrated remarkable intellectual determination. He taught himself to read and write, eventually attending Merritt College, where he became deeply engaged with political activism and revolutionary literature. During his time at Merritt College, Newton was profoundly influenced by emerging Black Power ideologies, Pan-African writings, and revolutionary texts. He developed close relationships with Bobby Seale and other activists who would become instrumental in forming the Black Panther Party.

Established on October 15th 1966, in Oakland, California, the Black Panther Party for Self Defense represented a radical departure from previous civil rights organizations. Newton and Seale developed an organizational structure that combined grassroots community service with revolutionary political ideology.

The party's ten point program outlined comprehensive demands;

1. Freedom and power to determine the destiny of the Black community

2. Full employment and decent housing

3. Complete exemption from military service

4. Immediate end to police brutality and murder of Black people

5. Constitutional right to self defense

6. Education that accurately represents Black historical experience

7. Immediate end to economic exploitation of the Black community

8. Decent housing fit for human beings

9. Exemption of Black men from all military service

10. Land, bread, housing, education, clothing, justice, and peace

Newton's leadership emphasized both armed self-defense and extensive community programs, including free breakfast for children, health clinics, and educational initiatives. The Black Panther Party's activism transcended traditional protest models. Their "survival programs" provided critical services to marginalized communities, challenging systemic inequalities through direct action. Free breakfast programs, health clinics, and educational workshops became hallmarks of their community centered approach. Newton articulated a theory of "revolutionary intercommunalism" that analyzed global power structures and advocated for solidarity among oppressed populations worldwide. The party developed alliances with other groups, including the American Indian Movement, Young Lords, and White Panther Party.

Newton's legal challenges became emblematic of state repression against Black revolutionary movements. He faced multiple legal battles, including a 1967 shootout with Oakland police that resulted in the death of an officer and Newton's subsequent imprisonment. His 1968 trial for the murder of police officer John Frey became a national cause celebre, with the "Free Huey" movement mobilizing widespread support. Newton was initially convicted of voluntary manslaughter but was later freed after a retrial.

Following his release from prison, Newton attempted to redirect the Black Panther Party's focus towards community service and electoral politics. However, internal conflicts, government repression, and personal challenges complicated these efforts. On August 22nd 1989, Newton was tragically murdered in West Oakland, a killing that shocked the activist community and symbolized the ongoing violence facing Black revolutionaries. Within days, Tyrone Robinson was arrested as a suspect; he was on parole and admitted the murder to police, claiming self-defense, though police found no evidence that Newton was carrying a gun. In 1991, Robinson was convicted of first degree murder and sentenced to a prison term of 32 years to life. His next parole hearing is set for November 2028. Robinson stated that his motive was to advance in the Black Guerrilla Family, a narcotics prison gang, in order to get a crack franchise.

Omar Assad

Omar Assad, also known as Omar As'ad, was a 78 year old Palestinian American who was born in the village of Jilijliya, located near Ramallah in the occupied West Bank. After spending many years in the United States, he returned to his home village in 2009 to enjoy his retirement. He was described by family members as a gentle and kind hearted man who cherished his family and community. The geopolitical situation in the region has been characterized by long standing tensions between Israelis and Palestinians. By 2022, the Israeli-Palestinian conflict remained unresolved, with ongoing disputes over territory, rights, and sovereignty. The occupation of Palestinian territories, including the West Bank, has led to numerous confrontations between Israeli forces and Palestinian civilians, creating an environment of mistrust and fear.

On January 12th 2022, Omar Assad was driving home after visiting friends when he encountered an Israeli military checkpoint in Jilijliya. He was stopped by Israeli soldiers who ordered him out of his vehicle. Witnesses reported that he was forcibly removed from his car. During his detention, Assad was handcuffed, blindfolded, and forced to lie face down on the ground. Reports indicate that he was left unresponsive for an extended period without medical assistance. The soldiers involved in the incident included members of the Israeli military unit known for its presence in the West Bank. The treatment Omar received during his detention raised serious concerns about the conduct of Israeli forces. Witnesses reported that he was treated harshly, which contributed to a lack of medical care during critical moments following his detention.

Prior to this incident, Omar Assad had no known serious health issues. Family members described him as being in good health for his age, actively participating in daily activities and maintaining a healthy lifestyle. Following his detention, Omar Assad suffered a stress induced cardiac arrest. An autopsy later revealed that his death resulted from a heart attack linked to the stress and physical abuse he endured while in custody. His family expressed devastation over his death, emphasizing that he was an innocent man who posed no threat to anyone.

The reaction from Omar Assad's family and community was one of outrage and grief. Family members demanded justice and accountability for the actions of Israeli soldiers that led to his death. Human rights organizations also condemned the incident, calling for an independent investigation into the circumstances surrounding Assad's death.

Gul Mudin

On January 15th 2010, Afghanistan was embroiled in a complex and protracted conflict involving U.S. military forces, NATO allies, and various insurgent groups. The U.S. had been involved in Afghanistan since 2001, following the September 11th attacks, with the primary objective of dismantling al-Qaeda and removing the Taliban from power. By 2010, the situation had evolved into a counterinsurgency effort aimed at stabilizing the country and building a functioning government. Interactions between U.S. military forces and local civilians were often fraught with tension. Despite efforts to win "hearts and minds," incidents involving civilian casualties frequently undermined these initiatives, leading to resentment and distrust among the Afghan population.

On January 15th 2010, in the village of La Mohammad Kalay in Kandahar Province, Gul Mudin, a 15 year old boy, was working on his family's farm when he became a victim of a tragic incident involving American soldiers from the 5th Stryker Brigade Combat Team. The soldiers involved included Jeremy Morlock, Andrew Holmes and Calvin Gibbs. They were part of a unit that had been deployed to conduct operations in the area against suspected Taliban fighters.

According to reports, as Gul Mudin was tending to his duties, he was approached by these soldiers. Under the direction of Staff Sergeant Calvin Gibbs,

Morlock and Holmes allegedly threw a grenade at Gul Mudin before shooting him multiple times. Following the attack, Morlock and Holmes took photographs with Gul Mudin's body and even cut off his little finger as a trophy. In a break with protocol, the soldiers also took photographs of themselves celebrating their kill. In the photos, Morlock grins and gives a thumbs up sign as he poses with Mudin's body. Staff Sgt. Calvin Gibbs reportedly used a pair of razor sharp medic's shears to cut off the fingers, which he presented to Holmes as a trophy for killing his first Afghan. According to a fellow soldier, Holmes took to carrying Mudin's severed fingers with him in a zip lock bag. "He wanted to keep the finger forever and wanted to dry it out," one of his friends would later report. "He was proud of his finger."

This incident was not isolated; it occurred against a backdrop of increasing tensions and frustrations among U.S. troops regarding their mission in Afghanistan. The incident sparked outrage both locally and internationally. Following an internal investigation by the U.S. Army, legal actions were taken against Morlock, Holmes, and Gibbs. Morlock was sentenced to 24 years in prison after pleading guilty to murder charges. Gibbs faced life imprisonment for his role in the killings. The killing of Gul Mudin intensified anti-American sentiment in Afghanistan and highlighted issues related to civilian casualties. Taking photos with Gul Mudin's body is indicative of a troubling detachment from the gravity of their actions. The collection of body parts as trophies reflects a disturbing moral decline within the ranks of the U.S. military.

- Holmes poses with Mudin's body.

Emmett Till

The murder of Emmett Till in 1955 serves as a pivotal moment in American history, particularly in the context of racial tensions prevalent in the Southern states during the 1950s. This period was marked by systemic racism, segregation, and violent reprisals against African Americans who dared to challenge the status quo. The Jim Crow laws enforced racial segregation and disenfranchised Black citizens, fostering an environment where acts of violence against them were often overlooked or justified. Till's brutal murder and the subsequent trial of his killers became a flashpoint for the burgeoning Civil Rights Movement. The graphic images of his mutilated body, widely circulated in the media, shocked the nation and galvanized both Black and white Americans to confront racial injustice. This case not only highlighted the deep seated racism in America but also served as a catalyst for organized civil rights activism.

Emmett Louis Till was born on July 25th 1941, in Chicago, Illinois, to Mamie Till and Louis Till. Raised in a middle class neighborhood on the South Side of Chicago, Emmett was known for his lively personality and sense of humor. He attended an all-Black school and was described as responsible and caring, often taking on household duties to support his working mother.

In August 1955, at the age of 14, Emmett traveled to Money, Mississippi, to visit relatives. His mother had cautioned him about the stark differences between life in Chicago and the racially charged atmosphere of Mississippi. Despite her warnings, Emmett's desire to connect with his Southern roots led him to this fateful trip. On August 24th 1955, while visiting Bryant's Grocery and Meat Market with relatives, Emmett allegedly whistled at Carolyn Bryant Donham, a white woman working at the store. This brief interaction would have catastrophic consequences. Carolyn later testified that Till had made inappropriate advances towards her, claiming he had grabbed her and used vulgar language. Four days later, Carolyn's husband Roy Bryant and his half-brother J.W. Milam kidnapped Till from his great-uncle's home. They brutally beat him before shooting him in the head and disposing of his body in the Tallahatchie River. The violence inflicted upon Till was emblematic of the extreme measures taken to enforce white supremacy in the South.

The trial of Roy Bryant and J.W. Milam began on September 19th 1955, in Sumner, Mississippi. The courtroom dynamics were heavily influenced by racial bias; an all-white jury was selected amidst an atmosphere of intimidation against Black witnesses. Carolyn Bryant's testimony played a critical role; however, it was riddled with inconsistencies and lacked corroboration. Despite evidence indicating their guilt, including eyewitness accounts of their abduction of Till, the jury acquitted Bryant and Milam after deliberating for just over an hour. The acquittal sent shockwaves through the African American community and highlighted the failures of a justice system that protected white perpetrators while denying justice to Black victims.

Emmett Till's murder became a rallying cry for civil rights activists across America. The graphic images from his open-casket funeral, organized by his mother Mamie Till Mobley, revealed the brutality of racial violence and ignited outrage among those who viewed them. This event marked a significant turning point; many who had previously remained passive began to actively engage in civil rights activism. The case influenced prominent civil rights leaders such as Medgar Evers and sparked protests demanding justice for Till. Just months after his murder, Rosa Parks' refusal to give up her seat on a Montgomery bus catalyzed the Montgomery Bus Boycott, further uniting activists in their struggle against segregation.

In recent years, renewed interest in Till's story has led to calls for justice and accountability regarding historical racial violence. In 2017, Carolyn Bryant Donham admitted that she had fabricated her testimony about Till's alleged advances, a revelation that has reignited discussions about truth and reconciliation in American history.

- Till's mother looks over his mutilated corpse. Mamie Till had insisted on an open casket funeral.

Nat Turner

Nat Turner, an enslaved Black carpenter and preacher, led a significant rebellion in Southampton County, Virginia, from August 21st to 23rd 1831. This uprising, known as Nat Turner's Rebellion or the Southampton Insurrection, was influenced by a complex interplay of social, political, and economic factors that shaped the lives of enslaved individuals in early 19th century America. The social environment of the antebellum South was characterized by a rigid racial hierarchy and systemic oppression of Black people. Enslaved individuals were denied basic human rights and subjected to brutal treatment. Turner, who was taught to read and interpret the Bible by his enslaver's son, believed he was divinely chosen to lead his people to freedom. His role as a preacher allowed him to gather followers and spread his message of resistance among both enslaved and free Black communities. Turner's vision was partly inspired by a series of celestial events, including a solar eclipse in 1831, which he interpreted as signs from God urging him to act against slavery. This belief in divine sanction for his actions galvanized his resolve and attracted followers who shared similar frustrations about their oppression.

The political landscape during this period was fraught with tension between pro-slavery and abolitionist sentiments. The aftermath of the American Revolution had led to increasing debates about slavery's morality and legality. However, in the South, slaveholders were determined to maintain their economic interests tied to slavery. The fear of insurrections loomed large over slaveholding communities, leading to stricter laws governing enslaved people and heightened vigilance against potential uprisings. Turner's rebellion occurred against this backdrop of escalating tensions. The immediate political response included a violent crackdown on suspected rebels and stricter enforcement of slave codes. Following the rebellion, Virginia's legislature debated the possibility of gradual emancipation but ultimately opted for harsher restrictions on enslaved people.

Economically, the Southern economy relied heavily on agriculture, particularly tobacco and cotton, which depended on slave labor. Enslavers viewed their human property as critical assets; thus, any threat to this system was met with severe repercussions. The rebellion not only threatened the lives of white plantation owners but also jeopardized their economic stability. In the wake of the uprising, white vigilantes killed dozens of Black people suspected of involvement or even mere association with Turner. This "reign of terror" not only decimated families but also instilled fear within the Black community, leading many free Black individuals to flee or go into hiding.

The rebellion also prompted discussions among white leaders about how to prevent future insurrections. They recognized that indiscriminate killings could undermine their economic interests by depleting their labor force. As a result, some measures were taken to limit violence against enslaved individuals while still maintaining oppressive control over them.

Nat Turner was captured on October 30th 1831, after evading authorities for nearly two months. His trial began on November 5th, where he was quickly convicted and sentenced to death. Turner was executed on November 11th 1831. His trial drew significant attention; it became a spectacle that highlighted the fears and anxieties of Southern whites regarding slave rebellions.

Razan al-Najjar

The Israeli-Palestinian conflict has persisted for decades, resulting in significant humanitarian crises, particularly affecting civilians and medical personnel. The ongoing hostilities have created a perilous environment for healthcare workers, who play a crucial role in providing medical assistance during times of conflict. Medical personnel are often on the front lines, risking their lives to care for the injured, yet they frequently face violence and hostility from military forces.

Razan al-Najjar was born on September 13th 1997, in Khuzaa, near Khan Younis, Gaza. Growing up in a family of six, she was motivated by a strong sense of duty to her community and a desire to help others. Despite facing financial challenges, she pursued her education and trained as a paramedic at Nasser Hospital. Razan became known for her bravery and commitment to humanitarian service, volunteering with the Palestinian Medical Relief Society (PMRS) during the Gaza protests. On June 1st 2018, during the Great March of Return, a series of protests demanding an end to the Israeli blockade and the right of return for Palestinian refugees, Razan was among the medical personnel deployed to assist injured demonstrators. On that day, thousands gathered near the Gaza-Israel border fence. Razan and her team were clearly marked as medics, wearing white vests and carrying medical supplies.

As they attempted to reach a wounded protester approximately 100 meters from the border fence, Razan was shot by an Israeli sniper. Eyewitness accounts indicate that she was not posing any threat at the time she was shot. Following the incident, she was rushed to a trauma stabilization point but succumbed to her injuries shortly after arriving at the hospital. The circumstances surrounding Razan's death have been widely debated. Initial claims from Israeli officials suggested that she may have been caught in crossfire or hit by ricochet. However, investigations by human rights organizations like B'Tselem concluded that she was deliberately targeted while performing her duties as a medic. Reports indicated that she posed no imminent threat to Israeli forces and was clearly identifiable as a healthcare worker.

Medical personnel operating in conflict zones face numerous risks, including physical harm from direct attacks and psychological trauma from witnessing violence. The actions of the IDF in Gaza have resulted in an environment where healthcare workers are frequently endangered. Since the inception of the Great March of Return in March 2018, there has been a significant increase in violence against medical staff. Over 1,300 health workers have reportedly been killed since 2018. Numerous incidents of injury among medical personnel have been documented during protests. A report by Insecurity Insight indicated that 138 Palestinian healthcare staff were killed between October 2023 and January 2024 alone.

Hani al-Jaafarawi

Hani al-Jaafarawi served as the Director of Ambulances and Emergency Services in Gaza City, playing a vital role in coordinating emergency medical responses during times of crisis. His significance as a leader in the healthcare sector made his work essential for the survival of many in Gaza. International humanitarian law (IHL), particularly the Geneva Conventions, provides essential protections for medical personnel in armed conflicts; medical personnel must not be targeted; they are entitled to respect and protection as long as they do not engage in hostilities, medical staff are required to treat all individuals without discrimination based on nationality, race, or political beliefs and parties to a conflict must ensure that medical personnel can access wounded individuals and provide necessary care without obstruction.

Despite these protections, numerous incidents have highlighted systemic violations against medical personnel in Palestine. Reports indicate that since October 2023, there have been over 1,300 documented attacks on healthcare workers and facilities in the occupied Palestinian territories (OPT).

Historically, medical personnel in Palestine have faced violence from military operations. Statistics reveal that over 1,300 paramedics and doctors have been killed since the escalation of hostilities began in October 2023. Case studies illustrate that attacks on ambulances and hospitals are not isolated incidents but part of a broader pattern aimed at undermining healthcare delivery.

On June 23rd 2024, an Israeli airstrike targeted the Daraj clinic in Gaza City, resulting in the death of Hani al-Jaafarawi and several others. The clinic was known for providing essential health services, including emergency care. The attack occurred amidst ongoing military operations that had escalated significantly in the region. The legality of the airstrike raises critical questions regarding compliance with international law. Human rights organizations have condemned such attacks as violations of IHL, which mandates protections for medical facilities. Eyewitness accounts reported that the clinic was clearly marked as a healthcare facility, yet it was struck without warning.

Iyad Rantisi

Research on the targeting of medical personnel in conflict zones highlights significant violations of international humanitarian law (IHL). The Geneva Conventions provide specific protections for medical staff, emphasizing their right to operate without fear of attack. However, numerous studies document systematic violence against healthcare workers in Palestine. For instance, reports indicate that over 1,300 medical personnel have been killed since the escalation of hostilities began on October 7th 2023. Previous documented cases include Dr. Adnan al-Bursh, who also died under torture while detained by Israeli forces. These incidents reflect broader trends of violence against healthcare professionals in conflict zones, where their safety is often compromised.

Iyad Rantisi was detained by Israeli forces on November 10th 2023, at a military checkpoint while attempting to move from northern to southern Gaza as part of an evacuation order issued by the Israeli military. He was arrested under suspicion of involvement in activities related to hostage situations. Following his arrest, he was transferred to Shikma Prison for interrogation. Dr. Rantisi died six days later under suspicious circumstances while in custody. Reports suggest that he suffered from torture and ill-treatment during his detention; claims supported by human rights organizations that have condemned such practices as violations of IHL.

Mahmoud Abu Nujaila

Medecins Sans Frontieres (MSF) plays a crucial role in providing medical care in conflict areas, including Gaza. MSF operates under the principles of impartiality and neutrality, aiming to deliver healthcare to those in need regardless of their background. The organization has been instrumental in addressing the healthcare needs of Palestinians amidst ongoing violence, often facing substantial risks themselves.

On November 21st 2023, Al-Awda Hospital was struck by an Israeli airstrike during a period of heightened military activity in northern Gaza. The attack resulted in significant destruction and loss of life, including that of Mahmoud Abu Nujaila, a physician known for his dedication to patient care. Eyewitness accounts indicate that the hospital was clearly marked as a medical facility at the time of the strike.

Mahmoud Abu Nujaila served as a senior physician at Al-Awda Hospital, where he was responsible for treating patients with various medical conditions exacerbated by the ongoing conflict. His contributions were vital during emergencies, as he worked tirelessly to provide care despite limited resources and constant threats to his safety.

The targeting of medical personnel and facilities raises serious legal and ethical concerns under international humanitarian law (IHL). The Geneva Conventions explicitly protect medical workers and facilities from attack unless they are being used for military purposes. The airstrike on Al-Awda Hospital constitutes a potential violation of these laws, prompting calls for accountability from human rights organizations.

Ahmad Al-Sahar

On November 21st 2023, Al-Awda Hospital in northern Gaza was struck by an Israeli airstrike that resulted in the deaths of Ahmad Al-Sahar and Mahmoud Abu Nujaila. Eyewitness accounts describe a chaotic scene as medical staff attempted to treat patients amidst the destruction caused by the bombing. Reports from Medecins Sans Frontieres (MSF) emphasized that the hospital was clearly marked as a medical facility at the time of the strike. Eyewitnesses recounted hearing loud explosions followed by panic among patients and staff. "We were treating patients when suddenly everything went dark," one nurse recalled. "There was no warning; we didn't know what was happening." MSF condemned the attack as a blatant violation of international humanitarian law, stating that hospitals should be safe havens for those seeking care.

Official reports from human rights organizations further corroborate these accounts, noting that such attacks contribute to a climate of fear among healthcare workers in Gaza. The implications of this incident extend beyond immediate casualties; it raises serious concerns about the safety of medical personnel in conflict zones. International organizations have called for accountability regarding attacks on healthcare facilities and personnel. The WHO has documented numerous violations against medical staff in Gaza since October 2023. Advocacy groups emphasize the need for independent investigations into these incidents to ensure accountability for those responsible.

Ziad Al-Tarari

Ziad Al-Tarari was a dedicated physician at Al-Awda Hospital, one of the few remaining functional hospitals in northern Gaza. Tragically, he was killed during an airstrike on November 21st 2023, which also claimed the lives of other medical professionals. Dr. Ziad Al-Tarari was a respected physician at Al-Awda Hospital in northern Gaza. He had extensive training and experience in emergency medicine and was known for his commitment to providing care under challenging conditions. His contributions were vital during crises, as he worked tirelessly alongside other medical staff to treat patients affected by ongoing violence.

On November 21st 2023, Al-Awda Hospital was struck by an Israeli airstrike during a period of heightened military activity in Gaza. Eyewitness accounts describe chaos as the hospital was hit while medical staff were attending to patients. MSF had previously communicated with warring parties regarding the hospital's status as a functioning medical facility, sharing its GPS coordinates to ensure its protection.

Larbi Ben M'hidi

The Algerian War of Independence was a pivotal conflict that marked Algeria's struggle against French colonial rule. This war was characterized by guerrilla warfare, extensive use of torture by the French, and a fierce determination among the Algerian people to achieve sovereignty. Amidst this tumultuous backdrop, one revolutionary figure emerged as a prominent leader; Larbi Ben M'hidi. Born on March 3rd 1923, in El Harrach, near Algiers, Ben M'hidi was deeply influenced by the socio-political climate of colonial Algeria. His early life, marked by a commitment to education and nationalism, laid the foundation for his future role in the fight for independence.

Larbi Ben M'hidi became a key figure in the National Liberation Front (FLN), which spearheaded the armed struggle against French colonialism. His contributions included organizing military operations and mobilizing support among the Algerian populace. Ben M'hidi was instrumental during significant events such as the Battle of Algiers in 1956-1957, where FLN fighters launched urban guerrilla attacks against French forces. His leadership not only galvanized fighters but also helped to articulate the political aspirations of the Algerian people amidst a backdrop of severe repression and violence. The political landscape during his involvement was fraught with tension. The French government responded to FLN actions with brutal counterinsurgency tactics, leading to widespread human rights abuses. Ben M'hidi's ability to navigate these treacherous waters and maintain morale among his comrades showcased his strategic acumen and unwavering commitment to Algeria's independence.

Ben M'hidi's revolutionary activities eventually led to his capture by French paratroopers on February 23rd 1957. The circumstances surrounding his arrest were controversial; he was reportedly betrayed by informants and arrested in an apartment while unarmed. Following his capture, he was subjected to intense interrogation techniques designed to extract information about FLN operations. Accounts from witnesses and fellow prisoners reveal that Ben M'hidi endured severe torture during his confinement. Despite this, he remained resolute, famously asserting that Algeria would ultimately prevail in its struggle for freedom. His dignity under duress earned him respect even from some of his captors, though it did not prevent the brutal treatment he received at their hands.

The events leading up to Ben M'hidi's execution are shrouded in controversy and conflicting narratives. He was declared dead on March 4th 1957, with official reports claiming he had committed suicide by hanging himself with strips torn from his shirt. However, many who knew him vehemently disputed this claim, citing his devout Muslim faith which forbids suicide as a central tenet. In later revelations, including admissions from former French military officials, it became clear that Ben M'hidi was executed following torture. His death had profound implications for the revolutionary movement; it served as a rallying cry for Algerians and highlighted the lengths to which colonial powers would go to suppress dissent.

Larbi Tbessi

Larbi Tbessi, also known as Larbi Ferhati, was a significant figure in Algeria's struggle for independence from French colonial rule. Born in 1891 in Cheria, Tebessa Province, he was raised in an environment that fostered a strong sense of nationalism and a commitment to reform. Tbessi's early education laid the groundwork for his later political activism, as he became increasingly aware of the injustices faced by Algerians under colonial rule.

The historical context leading up to the Algerian War of Independence was marked by a series of events that heightened nationalist sentiments. Algeria had been under French control since 1830, and the oppressive policies enacted by the colonial government led to widespread discontent. The aftermath of World War II saw increased calls for independence, culminating in violent confrontations such as the Setif and Guelma massacre in 1945, where thousands of Algerians were killed by French forces in response to protests demanding independence.

Tbessi's political activism began in earnest during the 1930s as he joined the Association of Algerian Muslim Ulema, an organization dedicated to promoting Algerian identity and advocating for reform. His involvement in this association positioned him as a key player in the nationalist movement. Tbessi's efforts included organizing educational initiatives and promoting cultural awareness, which were crucial for fostering a sense of unity among Algerians.

In 1943, Tbessi was imprisoned due to his political activities, reflecting the French authorities' increasing intolerance towards dissent. He was released after a year but was soon re-arrested following the violent repression of the Setif and Guelma massacre. This event marked a turning point in the Algerian independence movement, as it galvanized many previously moderate Algerians to adopt more radical positions against colonial rule.

On April 4th 1957, Larbi Tbessi was arrested at his home in Algiers by disguised paratroopers. The circumstances surrounding his arrest remain murky, with reports indicating that he was taken without due process amid a broader crackdown on FLN activists during the war. His disappearance had significant implications for the independence movement; it underscored the brutal tactics employed by French forces to suppress dissent and instilled fear among other activists. The lack of information regarding his fate further fueled resentment against French colonial rule and motivated many to intensify their commitment to the struggle for independence. Tbessi's status as a missing person became emblematic of the countless individuals who disappeared during this tumultuous period.

Larbi Tbessi ultimately met a tragic end at the hands of French Army commandos in 1957. Reports indicate that he was brutally executed; his body was burned in hot oil, a method intended to obliterate any trace of his remains. The French authorities' refusal to return his body to Algeria has been interpreted as an attempt to erase his memory and diminish his significance within the nationalist narrative.

The manner of Tbessi's death has had lasting repercussions on contemporary Algerian society. It served as a rallying point for nationalists who viewed him as a martyr for the cause of independence. His legacy is reflected in Algeria's collective memory; figures like Tbessi are commemorated as symbols of resistance against oppression and injustice.

Ruben Um Nyobe

The historical context of Cameroon during the colonial period is marked by a complex interplay of power dynamics and cultural upheaval. Following World War I, Cameroon was divided between French and British colonial rule, leading to significant political and social unrest among the indigenous population. Amidst this backdrop, Ruben Um Nyobe emerged as a key figure in the anti-colonialist movement. As the leader of the Union of the Peoples of Cameroon (UPC), he played an instrumental role in advocating for independence from French colonial rule. His assassination on September 13th 1958, not only marked a tragic end to his life but also served as a catalyst for the independence movement, galvanizing support for the cause he championed.

Um Nyobe was born on April 10th 1913, in Song Mpeck, a village in what was then French Cameroon. His early education took place in Presbyterian missionary schools, where he developed a keen awareness of social injustices and colonial exploitation. After completing his schooling, he pursued further education and became a teacher. However, his political awakening truly began when he joined the colonial civil service in 1935. It was during this time that he witnessed firsthand the inequities perpetuated by French colonial policies.

In 1948, Um Nyobe played a crucial role in founding the Cameroon National Union (CNU), which later evolved into the UPC. His political ideology was rooted in a vision of a unified and independent Cameroon that prioritized social justice and economic equity for all citizens. He believed that true independence could only be achieved through collective action and political mobilization. Um Nyobe's strategies in the fight against French colonial rule were multifaceted. He initially advocated for non-violent resistance, drawing inspiration from global anti-colonial movements. His leadership within the UPC emphasized mass mobilization and grassroots organization to raise awareness about the plight of Cameroonians under colonial oppression. Key events during his tenure included his speeches at the United Nations General Assembly in 1952 and 1954, where he denounced French colonialism and called for immediate independence for Cameroon. These appearances positioned him as a prominent voice against colonial rule and highlighted his commitment to international advocacy.

However, as tensions escalated between the UPC and colonial authorities, Um Nyobe adapted his approach to include armed resistance. Following the banning of the UPC in 1955 by French authorities, who accused it of inciting rebellion, Um Nyobe went underground to continue organizing resistance efforts. He established the Kamerun National Liberation Army (ALNK), which engaged in armed struggle against French forces.

On September 13th 1958, Um Nyobe was assassinated by French military forces while hiding in a forest near Boumnyebel. The circumstances surrounding his death were brutal; he was shot during a military operation aimed at eliminating UPC leadership. The French military justified their actions by portraying Um Nyobe as a terrorist threat to national security. The immediate aftermath of his assassination dealt a severe blow to the Cameroonian independence movement. While it disrupted UPC activities temporarily, it did not extinguish the desire for independence among Cameroonians. Instead, Um Nyobe's death became a rallying point for nationalists who viewed him as a martyr for their cause.

Felix Roland Moumie

Felix Roland Moumie was a pivotal figure in Cameroon's anti-colonialist movement, known for his leadership in the Union des Populations du Cameroun (UPC). His activism emerged against a backdrop of colonial oppression and socio-political upheaval, as Cameroon transitioned from a French colony to an independent nation in 1960. Moumie's significance lies not only in his efforts to liberate Cameroon from colonial rule but also in his broader vision for African unity and independence, which continues to resonate in contemporary discussions about post-colonial identity.

Cameroon was colonized by Germany in the late 19th century but was later divided between France and Britain after World War I. The League of Nations mandated France to govern the larger part of Cameroon, leading to significant socio-economic changes and the imposition of colonial rule characterized by exploitation and repression. The struggle for independence gained momentum after World War II, particularly as nationalist sentiments spread across Africa.

In 1960, following years of political agitation and conflict, Cameroon achieved independence from France. However, this transition was fraught with challenges, including internal divisions and the lingering effects of colonial policies that had fostered tribalism and social fragmentation. The political landscape of Cameroon during the late 1950s was marked by the rise of nationalist movements advocating for independence. The UPC emerged as a leading force, calling for immediate self-governance and opposing the French administration's oppressive tactics. The assassination of UPC leader Ruben Um Nyobe in 1958 created a power vacuum that Moumie sought to fill, intensifying the struggle against colonial rule.

Moumie's political career began with his involvement in the UPC, founded in 1948 as a response to colonial injustices. After Nyobe's assassination, Moumie became the party leader and shifted its strategy towards more militant forms of resistance. He advocated for the unification of British and French Cameroons and sought to mobilize support from other African nations. Under Moumie's leadership, the UPC organized protests, strikes, and armed resistance against French forces. His charisma and commitment to anti-colonial ideals garnered him respect both domestically and internationally. He actively sought alliances with other African leaders and movements, emphasizing pan-African solidarity.

He rallied support for the UPC across Africa, emphasizing the need for unity against colonial powers. He represented Cameroonian interests at international forums, including the United Nations. Moumie envisioned a Cameroon free from tribal divisions, advocating for equitable governance and social justice.

On November 3rd 1960, while in Geneva for a meeting with other African leaders, Moumie was assassinated by an agent of the French secret service (SDECE). The assassin posed as a journalist and poisoned Moumie's drink with thallium during their meeting. This act was part of a broader strategy by France to eliminate threats to its colonial interests in Africa.

The SDECE's involvement highlights France's willingness to resort to extrajudicial measures to suppress anti-colonial movements. The assassination was part of France's "dirty war" against nationalists in Cameroon, where brutal tactics were employed to maintain control over its colonies. Following his death, Swiss authorities faced pressure not to pursue an investigation into the circumstances surrounding Moumie's assassination.

Heloise Ruth

The historical context of apartheid in South Africa is marked by systemic racial segregation and oppression established by the National Party after its rise to power in 1948. This regime enforced laws that marginalized non-white populations, leading to widespread resistance and activism. Among the notable figures in the anti-apartheid movement was Heloise Ruth First, a journalist, scholar, and activist whose life and work epitomized the struggle against oppression. Born on May 4th 1925, in Johannesburg to Latvian Jewish immigrants, First was influenced by her family's political activism and her education at the University of the Witwatersrand. Her early experiences shaped her motivations for activism, driving her to expose injustices and advocate for social change.

Ruth First's involvement in anti-apartheid movements began during her university years when she co-founded the Federation of Progressive Students. She became a prominent figure in the South African Congress of Democrats and later joined the African National Congress (ANC) and the South African Communist Party (SACP). Her journalistic career included significant contributions to newspapers like The Guardian and New Age, where she highlighted the brutal realities of apartheid through investigative reporting.

First participated actively in this 1952 campaign, which aimed to challenge unjust laws through civil disobedience. In 1956, she was among 156 activists tried for treason; although acquitted, this experience underscored the regime's repressive tactics. In 1963, First was detained under South Africa's 90 day detention law, spending 117 days in solitary confinement. Her account of this experience was published as 117 Days, providing a harrowing insight into state repression. First's writings addressed social justice and human rights issues extensively. Her articles exposed labor exploitation, racial discrimination, and the government's violent suppression of dissent. Through her journalism, she played a crucial role in mobilizing public opinion against apartheid.

Ruth First's academic career flourished during her exile from South Africa. After relocating to England in 1964, she published several influential works that analyzed the socio-political landscape of apartheid. Her research focused on topics such as labor relations, political violence, and the dynamics of revolutionary movements.

Notable publications include:

*The Barrel of a Gun: The Politics of Coups d'Etat in Africa, which examined military coups across the continent.

*Libya: The Elusive Revolution, providing insights into revolutionary movements.

*Black Gold: The Mozambican Miner (published posthumously), which analyzed migrant labor practices.

Through her scholarship, First contributed significantly to understanding apartheid's impact on South African society and provided a critical framework for analyzing resistance movements.

After leaving South Africa in 1964, Ruth First faced numerous challenges as an exile. Despite these difficulties, she remained committed to anti-apartheid activism. In Mozambique, where she relocated in 1977, First took on a role as research director at the Centre for African Studies at Eduardo Mondlane University. She continued to write and lecture on issues related to apartheid while supporting liberation movements from abroad. Her exile did not diminish her influence; instead, it expanded her reach as she collaborated with various organizations advocating for social justice. She worked closely with the ANC and SACP to provide support for anti-apartheid efforts within South Africa.

On August 17th 1982, Ruth First was assassinated by a parcel bomb sent by agents of the South African government. This act was part of a broader campaign against anti-apartheid activists living abroad. The circumstances surrounding her assassination highlighted the lengths to which the apartheid regime would go to silence dissent. The implications of her assassination were profound. It galvanized international condemnation of apartheid policies. It underscored the dangers faced by activists fighting against oppressive regimes. Her death served as a rallying point for further mobilization within anti-apartheid circles globally. Local and international communities mourned her loss, recognizing her contributions to journalism and activism.

Shireen Abu Akleh

Journalism plays a critical role in conflict zones, serving as a vital source of information and a means of accountability. In Palestine, the risks faced by journalists are particularly acute due to the ongoing Israeli-Palestinian conflict. Journalists often find themselves in perilous situations, where their safety is compromised by military actions, political tensions, and systemic violence. The case of Shireen Abu Akleh, a prominent Palestinian-American journalist killed on May 11th 2022, while covering an Israel Defense Forces (IDF) raid in the Jenin refugee camp, exemplifies the dangers journalists face in this volatile region.

The history of journalism in Palestine is deeply intertwined with the Israeli-Palestinian conflict, which has persisted for decades. Journalists in Palestine have historically faced censorship, violence, and intimidation from various actors, including state forces and militant groups. The media landscape is characterized by a struggle for narrative control, where journalists often operate under significant constraints and risks.

The IDF plays a pivotal role in shaping the media environment in Palestine. While it maintains that it does not target journalists intentionally, numerous reports indicate that military operations often result in casualties among media personnel. The relationship between the IDF and the media is complex; journalists are frequently caught between their duty to report and the realities of military engagement that can endanger their lives.

On May 11th 2022, Shireen Abu Akleh was shot while covering an IDF raid in Jenin. Eyewitness accounts state that she was clearly identified as a journalist at the time of her death. Reports indicate that she was struck by a single bullet to the head from Israeli forces. Eyewitnesses described a chaotic scene where Abu Akleh was shot despite wearing a press vest. Media organizations quickly condemned her killing, calling for an independent investigation into the circumstances surrounding her death. Various news outlets highlighted discrepancies between official IDF statements and eyewitness accounts. The response to Abu Akleh's death was swift and widespread. Local communities mourned her loss as she was a beloved figure in Palestinian journalism. Internationally, human rights organizations and media advocacy groups demanded accountability from Israeli authorities. The incident sparked protests and calls for justice across social media platforms.

Abu Akleh's death raised significant concerns about press freedom in Palestine. It underscored the dangers journalists face while reporting on military actions and heightened fears regarding self-censorship among reporters operating in conflict zones. The IDF's response to calls for accountability has been criticized as insufficient. Although investigations were promised, many observers argue that they lack transparency and fail to hold perpetrators accountable for attacks on journalists.

Issam Abdallah

The safety of journalists in conflict zones is a pressing issue that has garnered increasing attention in recent years. In regions like Palestine, where political tensions and military confrontations are prevalent, journalists face numerous risks while attempting to report on critical events. The Israel Defense Forces (IDF) play a significant role in this dynamic, often being implicated in attacks against media personnel. The Israeli-Palestinian conflict has a long and complex history that has significantly impacted journalists operating in the region. Since the establishment of Israel in 1948, various military operations have been conducted, resulting in numerous casualties among journalists.

According to the Committee to Protect Journalists (CPJ), at least 158 journalists have been killed during the ongoing conflict as of October 2024, with 133 being Palestinian. The majority of these fatalities occurred due to Israeli airstrikes or direct military actions. This alarming trend highlights the systemic risks faced by journalists in Palestine, where their safety is often compromised.

Issam Abdallah was a prominent journalist known for his coverage of conflicts in the Middle East. On October 13th 2023, he was killed during Israeli airstrikes while reporting on escalating tensions between Israel and Hezbollah in Southern Lebanon. Eyewitness accounts suggest that Abdallah was clearly identifiable as a journalist at the time of his death, raising serious concerns about the intentional targeting of media personnel.

Abdallah had built a reputation for his commitment to uncovering the truth behind conflicts affecting Palestinian communities. His work provided invaluable insights into the realities faced by civilians amid military operations. The implications of his death extend beyond personal loss; it signifies a broader threat to press freedom and the safety of journalists operating in volatile regions. The killing of Issam Abdallah reverberated throughout the international journalism community. Advocacy organizations such as Reporters Without Borders and CPJ condemned his death and called for accountability from Israeli authorities. His death has raised awareness about the dangers faced by journalists covering conflicts and highlighted the urgent need for protective measures.

Ismail Al Ghoual

Ismail Al Ghoual was a dedicated journalist working for Al Jazeera, known for his commitment to reporting on the realities faced by Palestinians. His work provided critical insights into the ongoing conflict and its impact on civilian populations.

On July 31st 2024, Ismail Al Ghoual was killed during an Israeli drone strike while covering an assassination attempt on Hamas leader Ismail Haniyah in Gaza City. Al Ghoual was reportedly relocating after a nearby building had been struck when he was hit by an airstrike that also resulted in civilian casualties. Eyewitness accounts indicate that he was clearly identifiable as a journalist at the time of his death.

The death of Ismail Al Ghoual sent shockwaves through the journalism community both locally and internationally. Advocacy organizations condemned his killing as part of a broader pattern of violence against journalists in Palestine. His death highlighted the urgent need for protective measures for media personnel operating in conflict zones and raised questions about accountability for such actions.

Approximately 75% of journalists were killed by Israeli airstrikes. The increasing number of journalist fatalities has profound implications for media coverage and public perception. The fear of violence can lead to self-censorship among reporters, limiting their ability to provide comprehensive coverage of events.

International humanitarian law provides protections for journalists operating in conflict zones. According to the Geneva Conventions, journalists are considered civilians and should not be targeted unless they directly participate in hostilities. The intentional killing of journalists is classified as a war crime.

Rami Al-Rifi

Rami Al-Rifi was a dedicated freelance photographer for Al Jazeera who was known for his commitment to reporting on the realities faced by Palestinians. On July 31st 2024, he was killed during an Israeli drone strike while covering an assassination attempt on Hamas leader Ismail Haniyah near Al-Shati refugee camp in Gaza City. Eyewitness accounts indicate that Al-Rifi and his colleague Ismail Al Ghoul were leaving the area after an initial strike hit a nearby building when their vehicle was targeted just minutes later.

Al-Rifi's work was significant for its focus on documenting military operations and their impact on civilian populations. His photography provided critical insights into the human cost of conflict and helped raise awareness about the situation in Gaza. His dedication to journalism exemplified the vital role that local reporters play in informing both local and international audiences about ongoing events. The killing of Rami Al-Rifi sent shockwaves through the journalism community both locally and internationally. Advocacy organizations condemned his death as part of a broader pattern of violence against journalists in Palestine. His death highlighted the urgent need for protective measures for media personnel operating in conflict zones and raised questions about accountability for such actions.

Despite international laws designed to protect journalists during armed conflicts, enforcement remains inadequate. The Geneva Conventions stipulate that journalists should be treated as civilians unless they directly participate in hostilities. However, violations are common, with many attacks on journalists in Palestine going unpunished.

The ongoing violence against journalists raises concerns about future reporting in Palestine. The potential chilling effect on journalists may result in less coverage of critical issues affecting Palestinian communities, further obscuring the realities on the ground from international audiences.

Shaker Aamer

Guantanamo Bay, established in January 2002, is a U.S. detention facility located on the island of Cuba, designed to hold individuals deemed "enemy combatants" during the War on Terror. It has become notorious for its controversial practices, including indefinite detention without trial and allegations of torture. Among the detainees was Shaker Aamer, a Saudi born British resident, who was captured in Afghanistan in November 2001 and held at Guantanamo Bay from February 2002 until his release in October 2015. Aamer's case serves as a poignant illustration of the complexities surrounding justice and human rights in the context of counterterrorism policies.

The geopolitical landscape during Aamer's detention was heavily influenced by the U.S. led War on Terror, initiated after the September 11th attacks in 2001. The legal framework surrounding these detentions often circumvented both U.S. and international law, allowing for practices that violate fundamental human rights principles.

Shaker Aamer was initially detained by Afghan forces in late 2001 while working for a charity. He was transferred to Guantanamo Bay on February 14th 2002, coinciding with the birth of his fourth child. Over the years, Aamer faced numerous legal challenges and was cleared for release in 2007; however, he remained detained for an additional eight years due to concerns that he had witnessed torture by U.S. and UK officials during his imprisonment. His prolonged detention raised significant questions about legal accountability and human rights protections.

Aamer's experience at Guantanamo included severe torture and inhumane treatment, such as beatings and prolonged solitary confinement. These actions not only contravene international human rights standards but also reflect a broader pattern of abuse within the facility, undermining U.S. claims to uphold human rights globally. The treatment Aamer endured has prompted calls for accountability and an independent inquiry into the involvement of UK officials in CIA led torture programs.

Throughout his detention, Aamer's case sparked significant legal battles and advocacy efforts from various human rights organizations. His lawyers fought tirelessly for his release, highlighting the lack of charges against him and the ethical implications of his continued detention. Public opinion played a crucial role in advocating for Aamer's freedom; notable figures, including politicians and activists, rallied support through petitions and demonstrations.

Shaker Aamer's case encapsulates critical issues surrounding justice and human rights within the context of Guantanamo Bay. His prolonged detention without charge raises fundamental questions about legal standards and accountability in counterterrorism practices.

Feroz Abbasi

Guantanamo Bay was established in January 2002 as part of the U.S. government's response to the War on Terror. Its intended purpose was to hold "enemy combatants" without the protections typically afforded under U.S. law. Feroz Abbasi, born in Uganda and raised in the UK, was captured by U.S. forces in Afghanistan in late 2001. His detention occurred within a legal and political environment characterized by a lack of transparency and due process for detainees, often described as being in a "legal black hole" where they could not challenge their detention effectively.

Feroz Abbasi was detained under accusations of being an al-Qaeda member involved in a "martyrdom mission." He was transported to Guantanamo Bay in January 2002, where he remained for over three years. During this time, Abbasi endured harsh conditions including solitary confinement and allegations of torture, such as physical abuse and psychological manipulation. Reports indicate that he faced severe mistreatment that contributed to long term psychological effects.

The legal framework governing Guantanamo detentions has been contentious, with policies allowing for indefinite detention without charge. Abbasi's legal representation faced numerous challenges, including limited access to evidence and legal counsel. By January 2005, Abbasi was cleared of all charges; however, his release highlighted significant flaws in the legal processes that allowed for his prolonged detention without just cause.

After his release in January 2005, Abbasi's life was profoundly impacted by his experiences at Guantanamo. He faced psychological challenges stemming from his treatment during detention, which affected his reintegration into society. His case has influenced public perception regarding the treatment of detainees and has prompted discussions about necessary reforms within U.S. counterterrorism policies.

Abbasi's case illustrates severe human rights violations that occurred at Guantanamo Bay, raising questions about compliance with international law. The treatment he received reflects systemic issues within the U.S. justice system that prioritize national security over individual rights. The international community has responded with condemnation of such practices, calling for accountability and reform.

Said Abasin

Said Abasin was detained by U.S. forces in Afghanistan in late 2001 while driving a taxi. He was transferred to Guantanamo Bay in early 2002, where he remained for over a year. During his detention, Abasin faced harsh conditions, including solitary confinement and various forms of torture aimed at extracting confessions and intelligence. Reports indicate that he was subjected to physical abuse and psychological manipulation, which severely impacted his mental health. Ultimately, after extensive legal proceedings, he was cleared of all charges by January 2005, highlighting the failures of the detention system.

The torture and wrongful detention experienced by Said Abasin exemplify significant human rights violations under international law. The United Nations Convention Against Torture explicitly prohibits such treatment, yet the practices at Guantanamo Bay often contravened this and other international treaties designed to protect individuals from cruel and inhumane treatment. The psychological and social impacts of wrongful detention extend beyond the individual to affect families and communities, perpetuating cycles of trauma.

The legal processes surrounding Guantanamo Bay have been marked by a lack of transparency and accountability. Detainees were often denied access to fair trials or adequate legal representation, raising concerns about due process violations. Efforts for accountability regarding human rights abuses have been met with resistance from various governmental entities, complicating attempts by organizations like Amnesty International and Human Rights Watch to advocate for reform.

Said Abasin's case reflects systemic issues within the U.S. military and legal systems that prioritize national security over individual rights. Public perception of detainees has been largely shaped by media representations that often dehumanize individuals held at Guantanamo Bay. This narrative can influence policy decisions and public support for continued detention practices without due process.

Mohammed al-Qahtani

The geopolitical climate following the September 11th attacks created a sense of urgency within the U.S. government to detain individuals suspected of terrorism. Mohammed al-Qahtani was allegedly intended to be the "20th hijacker" in the 9/11 attacks but was turned away from entering the U.S. in August 2001 due to suspicions about his intentions. After being captured in Afghanistan during the Battle of Tora Bora, he was transferred to Guantanamo Bay, where he became one of the most notorious cases associated with torture and wrongful detention.

During al-Qahtani's detention at Guantanamo Bay, he faced severe conditions and a lack of legal protections typical for detainees at the facility. Initially classified as an "enemy combatant," al-Qahtani was subjected to aggressive interrogation techniques that included prolonged isolation, sleep deprivation, and physical and psychological abuse. Reports indicate that he endured systematic torture as part of a coordinated effort approved by high ranking officials, including then-Secretary of Defense Donald Rumsfeld.

International law defines torture as any act that inflicts severe pain or suffering for purposes such as obtaining information or punishment. In al-Qahtani's case, methods included sexual humiliation, exposure to extreme temperatures, and threats with military dogs. The psychological impact of such treatment has been profound; al-Qahtani exhibited signs of severe mental health deterioration during his detention, which were exacerbated by the torture he endured. His experiences highlight the long term consequences of torture on individuals' mental and physical health.

Al-Qahtani's legal journey involved various military commissions and attempts to challenge his detention. Despite being charged with war crimes, including conspiracy to commit murder, his case was complicated by the fact that much of the evidence against him was obtained through torture, rendering it inadmissible in court. Ultimately, a review board determined that his continued detention was no longer necessary for national security, leading to his release in March 2006.

The implications of al-Qahtani's case extend beyond his personal experience; they raise critical questions about U.S. foreign policy and human rights practices. His wrongful detention has contributed to growing public criticism regarding Guantanamo Bay and its treatment of detainees. Al-Qahtani's case serves as a cautionary tale about the dangers of prioritizing security over justice and civil liberties.

Frank Teruggi

A whistleblower is an individual who exposes information or activities within an organization that are deemed illegal, unethical, or not in the public interest. Whistleblowers play a critical role in promoting transparency and accountability, often at great personal risk. Their disclosures can lead to significant changes in policies and practices, thereby safeguarding public interest.

Frank Teruggi was an American journalist and activist who became a victim of political repression during the military dictatorship of General Augusto Pinochet in Chile. Born in 1949, Teruggi was involved in anti-Vietnam War activism and moved to Chile to support President Salvador Allende's socialist government. His commitment to uncovering human rights abuses ultimately led to his abduction and execution on September 30th 1973, shortly after the military coup that overthrew Allende.

The Pinochet regime emerged from a violent coup on September 11th 1973, which resulted in the overthrow of the democratically elected government of Salvador Allende. The regime was characterized by widespread human rights violations, including torture, forced disappearances, and extrajudicial killings. Political dissent was met with brutal repression as the military sought to consolidate power and eliminate opposition.

In authoritarian contexts like Pinochet's Chile, journalism serves as a vital check on power but comes with substantial risks. Journalists often face censorship, intimidation, and violence for reporting on government abuses. The case of Frank Teruggi exemplifies the dangers faced by journalists who dare to expose the truth about human rights violations.

Frank Teruggi was an active member of the Industrial Workers of the World (IWW) and worked for a small newsletter called FIN (Fuente de Informacion Norteamericano) in Santiago. His journalism focused on documenting U.S. involvement in Chilean politics and advocating for human rights amidst growing political tensions.

On September 20th 1973, just nine days after the coup, Teruggi was arrested by the Chilean military at his home. He was taken to the National Stadium in Santiago, which had been repurposed as a detention center where many were tortured and executed. Despite being a U.S. citizen, he was not spared from the regime's brutality.

Teruggi's body was discovered two weeks later at a morgue, bearing signs of torture and gunshot wounds. His death underscored the lethal risks faced by journalists during this period and highlighted the complicity of U.S. intelligence in his murder, as declassified documents later revealed that U.S. officials had monitored his activities.

The assassination of Frank Teruggi sent shockwaves through the journalistic community both in Chile and internationally. It served as a grim reminder of the dangers faced by those who challenge authoritarian regimes and highlighted the urgent need for protective measures for journalists. Teruggi's case is emblematic of the broader risks faced by whistleblowers globally. It illustrates how authoritarian governments often resort to violence to silence dissenting voices, which can deter future whistleblowers from coming forward with critical information about human rights abuses.

Frank Teruggi's fate parallels that of other whistleblowers who have faced violent repercussions for their actions. For instance, Charles Horman, another American journalist killed shortly after Teruggi, also exposed U.S. complicity in human rights abuses during the Pinochet regime. Similarly, cases like those of journalist Anna Politkovskaya in Russia or environmental activist Berta Caceres in Honduras showcase common patterns; targeting individuals who threaten powerful interests through their revelations.

Charles Horman

Born on May 15th 1942, Charles Horman was a filmmaker who moved to Chile in 1971 to document the social and political changes under President Salvador Allende's socialist government. His work aimed to highlight the human rights situation and the effects of U.S. intervention in Chilean politics. Horman's dedication to revealing the truth about human rights abuses would lead him into grave danger during the military coup that occurred on September 11th 1973.

In the early 1970s, Chile was marked by deep political polarization and economic instability. President Allende's government faced opposition from various sectors, including business elites and segments of the military. The situation escalated as tensions rose between Allende's socialist policies and U.S. interests in Latin America, which viewed his government as a threat to democracy and capitalism.

The United States played a significant role in Chilean politics during this period, particularly through covert operations conducted by the CIA aimed at destabilizing Allende's government. This included funding opposition groups and supporting military leaders who opposed Allende. The culmination of these efforts was the coup on September 11th 1973, which resulted in Allende's overthrow and marked the beginning of General Augusto Pinochet's brutal dictatorship.

Horman's documentary filmmaking focused on capturing the realities of life under Allende's administration, emphasizing social justice and human rights issues. His work aimed to provide a counter-narrative to mainstream portrayals of socialism in Latin America. Through his films, Horman sought to raise awareness about the human rights violations occurring in Chile. His commitment to documenting these issues contributed to a broader understanding of U.S. involvement in Latin America and its consequences for ordinary citizens.

On September 17th 1973, just days after the coup, Horman was abducted by soldiers from his home in Santiago. He was taken to the National Stadium, which had been converted into a detention center where many were tortured and executed. His wife, Joyce Horman, reported his disappearance to U.S. officials but faced bureaucratic hurdles and indifference from embassy personnel. Horman was executed shortly after his abduction on September 19, 1973. His body was later discovered buried within a wall at the stadium. Investigations revealed that U.S. intelligence had provided information that likely led to his identification as a "subversive," resulting in his execution.

Horman's murder elicited outrage both domestically and internationally. It raised critical questions about U.S. complicity in human rights abuses under Pinochet's regime and highlighted the dangers faced by journalists and whistleblowers who expose uncomfortable truths.

Orlando Letelier

Orlando Letelier, a former Chilean ambassador to the United States and a prominent critic of the Pinochet regime, exemplifies the peril faced by whistleblowers who expose uncomfortable truths. His life and tragic assassination underscore the dangers associated with standing up against oppressive regimes.

Orlando Letelier was born on April 13th 1932, in Santiago, Chile. He served as a key figure in Salvador Allende's government, holding positions such as ambassador to the United States and minister of foreign affairs. Following the military coup led by General Augusto Pinochet on September 11th 1973, Letelier was arrested, tortured, and later released due to international pressure. He sought refuge in the U.S., where he became an outspoken advocate against human rights abuses perpetrated by the Pinochet regime.

The political landscape in Chile during Pinochet's rule was marked by severe repression. Following the coup that ousted Allende, thousands were killed or disappeared as the military government sought to eliminate dissent. The regime employed widespread torture and extrajudicial killings to maintain control over the populace.

During this period, human rights abuses were rampant, with organizations like the National Commission on Political Imprisonment and Torture documenting these violations. Whistleblowers played a crucial role in bringing these issues to light, often risking their lives to expose the truth about state sponsored violence and repression. Letelier's efforts to highlight these abuses positioned him as a significant threat to the regime.

Letelier used his platform in exile to raise awareness about the atrocities committed under Pinochet's rule. He engaged with various media outlets and spoke at international forums to shed light on human rights violations in Chile. His work included publishing articles and giving speeches that detailed the systematic torture and killings carried out by the regime. One notable event was his impassioned speech at Madison Square Garden on September 10th 1976, where he addressed a large audience about the ongoing repression in Chile. This public engagement helped galvanize international support for Chilean exiles and increased scrutiny of U.S. foreign policy towards Latin America.

On September 21st 1976, Letelier was assassinated in Washington, D.C., by a car bomb planted by agents of DINA (Direccion de Inteligencia Nacional), the Chilean secret police. He was driving with his assistant Ronni Moffitt when the bomb exploded, killing both instantly and injuring Moffitt's husband. The assassination was part of Operation Condor, a coordinated effort among South American dictatorships to eliminate political opponents abroad. Letelier's assassination had profound implications for U.S.-Chilean relations and highlighted the extent of state sponsored terrorism employed by Pinochet's regime. It underscored the vulnerability of political exiles even in countries like the United States that were ostensibly committed to human rights.

The assassination elicited widespread international condemnation. Human rights organizations and foreign governments denounced the act as a blatant violation of sovereignty and human rights. The incident marked a turning point in U.S.-Latin American relations, prompting calls for a reassessment of support for authoritarian regimes. In response to Letelier's assassination, some U.S. officials began advocating for a more aggressive stance against Pinochet's government. Declassified documents reveal that State Department officials pushed for policies aimed at forcing Pinochet from power due to his regime's violent actions against dissidents.

Orlando Letelier's legacy continues to resonate within human rights activism today. His commitment to exposing injustices serves as an inspiration for current whistleblowers who face similar risks in their pursuit of truth. His assassination highlighted the need for stronger protections for those who dare to speak out against oppressive regimes.

John McCarthy

John McCarthy was an environmental engineer who worked at a nuclear facility in the United States. He was motivated by a strong sense of ethics and responsibility to protect public health and safety. McCarthy became increasingly concerned about the facility's practices, which he believed endangered both workers and the surrounding community. During his tenure, McCarthy uncovered several significant environmental violations, including improper waste disposal and inadequate safety measures that could lead to catastrophic accidents. His findings indicated that radioactive materials were being mishandled, posing serious risks to both public health and the environment. McCarthy documented these violations meticulously, intending to bring them to light through official channels.

On February 12th 1980, John McCarthy died in a suspicious car accident that many believe was orchestrated to silence him. The circumstances surrounding his death raised numerous questions, particularly given his recent whistleblowing activities. Eyewitness accounts suggested that his car had been tampered with prior to the accident, leading to speculation about foul play. Investigations into McCarthy's death revealed inconsistencies in police reports and witness testimonies that pointed toward possible sabotage. Media coverage at the time highlighted these discrepancies, fueling public suspicion regarding the true nature of his death.

Despite these concerns, official investigations concluded that it was merely an accident, leaving many unanswered questions about the potential involvement of powerful interests in his demise.

McCarthy's revelations had immediate repercussions on nuclear safety protocols in the United States. Following his disclosures, regulatory agencies began implementing stricter safety measures and oversight procedures at nuclear facilities nationwide. His efforts helped expose systemic flaws within the industry and prompted calls for reform. In the wake of McCarthy's whistleblowing, several pieces of legislation were introduced aimed at enhancing safety standards in the nuclear industry. These changes included increased funding for safety inspections and more stringent penalties for violations, reflecting a growing recognition of the importance of accountability within high stakes industries.

Karen Silkwood

One of the most notable cases in the history of whistleblowing is that of Karen Silkwood, a chemical technician and labor union activist who worked at the Kerr-McGee plutonium processing plant in Crescent, Oklahoma. Silkwood's efforts to expose unsafe working conditions and contamination risks ultimately led to her tragic death under suspicious circumstances. Her story not only highlights the dangers faced by whistleblowers but also underscores the need for robust protections for those who dare to speak out against powerful interests.

During the 1970s, the plutonium processing industry was burgeoning due to increasing interest in nuclear energy as a viable alternative to fossil fuels. The Kerr-McGee Corporation operated one of the key facilities in this sector, producing plutonium fuel rods for nuclear reactors. However, this rapid expansion often came at the expense of safety and regulatory compliance. At this time, safety standards and regulations governing nuclear facilities were often inadequate. The Atomic Energy Commission (AEC) was responsible for overseeing safety protocols; however, enforcement was lax, and many facilities prioritized production over worker safety. Reports of contamination incidents and health violations were common, yet little action was taken to address these concerns. The implications for worker safety were dire, as employees like Silkwood faced exposure to hazardous materials without adequate protection or oversight.

Karen Silkwood began her career at Kerr-McGee in 1972 and quickly became aware of serious safety violations within the plant. She observed numerous instances of contamination, including spills of radioactive materials and inadequate safety measures that put workers at risk. Silkwood documented these issues meticulously, noting that workers were frequently exposed to high levels of plutonium without proper training or protective equipment. Silkwood's commitment to exposing these unsafe practices led her to join the Oil, Chemical, and Atomic Workers Union (OCAW), where she became a member of the union's negotiating team; the first woman to hold this position at Kerr-McGee. In 1974, she testified before the AEC about her concerns regarding health and safety violations at the plant. Silkwood also began gathering evidence to support her claims, including documents and photographs that detailed the extent of contamination risks. Her determination to expose these issues culminated in a meeting with a New York Times reporter on November 13th 1974, during which she intended to provide evidence of Kerr-McGee's negligence. Tragically, she never made it to that meeting.

On November 13th 1974, Karen Silkwood died in a suspicious car accident while driving to meet with the reporter. She had been under immense pressure due to her whistleblowing activities and had expressed fears about her safety in the days leading up to her death.

Silkwood's car crashed into a concrete culvert after she reportedly swerved off the road. The official investigation concluded that she had fallen asleep at the wheel; however, many questioned this narrative given her recent activities and concerns about contamination. Witnesses reported seeing her distressed prior to her departure from a union meeting earlier that evening. The circumstances surrounding her death have led to numerous theories regarding foul play. Some speculate that she may have been deliberately targeted due to her whistleblowing efforts. Investigations into her death revealed inconsistencies in police reports and raised questions about whether she had been sabotaged.

Carlos Alberto Lopes Cardoso

Carlos Alberto Lopes Cardoso, known as Carlos Cardoso, was a prominent investigative journalist from Mozambique whose work significantly impacted the country's media landscape and political accountability. Born on August 10th 1951, in Beira to Portuguese immigrant parents, Cardoso became a key figure in uncovering corruption in Mozambique, particularly during the late 1990s and early 2000s, a period marked by political transition and economic challenges following the end of the civil war in 1992.

During this time, Mozambique experienced rapid economic growth, largely driven by foreign investment and structural reforms. However, this growth was shadowed by widespread corruption and governance issues, particularly surrounding the privatization of state owned enterprises. Cardoso's investigations into these matters not only revealed the depths of corruption but also highlighted the critical role of a free press in fostering accountability.

Carlos Cardoso's early life was shaped by the political turbulence of colonial Mozambique. He completed his secondary education in South Africa, where he became involved in anti-apartheid activism. This activism led to his deportation back to Mozambique just before the country gained independence from Portuguese rule in 1975. Following independence, Cardoso worked in various government media roles before becoming an editor at the government press agency AIM.

In 1989, after a brief imprisonment for his outspoken views, he left AIM to pursue independent journalism. He founded Mediacoop, an independent press cooperative, and later established the weekly newspaper Savana in 1992. His commitment to journalistic integrity and accountability set the stage for his later investigative work into corruption.

Cardoso's most significant investigations centered on the privatization of Banco Comercial de Moçambique (BCM), Mozambique's largest bank. His reporting uncovered a massive fraud scheme involving $14 million that occurred just before the bank's privatization in 1996. This scandal implicated high-level officials and powerful business figures, leading Cardoso to demand accountability for those involved. His findings played a crucial role in raising public awareness about corruption within the government and financial institutions. By exposing these issues through his articles, Cardoso not only informed the public but also pressured authorities to take action against corrupt practices.

On November 22nd 2000, Carlos Cardoso was assassinated in Maputo while investigating ongoing corruption linked to BCM. His murder shocked the nation and raised alarms about press freedom in Mozambique. The investigation into his death revealed connections to powerful individuals, including Nyimpine Chissano, son of then President Joaquim Chissano. The circumstances surrounding his assassination suggested that it was motivated by his relentless pursuit of truth and accountability.

Public outcry followed his death, both domestically and internationally, with calls for justice highlighting the dangers faced by journalists in Mozambique.

Cardoso's assassination had profound implications for journalism in Mozambique. It underscored the risks that investigative journalists face when exposing corruption and holding people in power accountable. In response to his death, there were increased discussions about media freedom and the need for protective measures for journalists. The public perception of journalism shifted as citizens recognized the importance of a free press in safeguarding democracy. However, it also instilled fear among journalists who faced potential repercussions for their work.

Anton Theodor Eberhard August Lubowski

Anton Lubowski was a prominent anti-apartheid activist and lawyer in Namibia, known for his unwavering commitment to social justice and human rights. Born on February 3rd 1953, Lubowski became a key figure in the South West Africa People's Organisation (SWAPO), advocating for the rights of all Namibians during a tumultuous period marked by apartheid. His activism included efforts to unite various racial groups against oppression and to promote a non-racial society. Tragically, Lubowski was assassinated on September 12th 1989, just months before Namibia's independence, in an attack orchestrated by the Civil Cooperation Bureau (CCB), a covert South African state organization. His death not only underscored the dangers faced by anti-apartheid activists but also highlighted the broader struggle against systemic racism in Southern Africa. Lubowski's legacy continues to influence contemporary activism in Namibia, serving as a reminder of the sacrifices made for freedom and justice.

Anton Theodor Eberhard August Lubowski was born into a prominent family in Luderitz, Namibia. His early life was marked by his education at Stellenbosch University and the University of Cape Town, where he studied law. Influenced by the socio-political injustices surrounding him, Lubowski became deeply involved in anti-apartheid activism, joining SWAPO in 1984 as its first white member. He fought tirelessly against racial discrimination and advocated for the rights of marginalized communities. During the apartheid era, Namibia was under South African administration, facing severe repression and violence against those who opposed the regime. The socio-political context was fraught with tension as SWAPO led the liberation struggle against colonial rule.

Existing literature on Anton Lubowski includes biographies and historical accounts that detail his life and activism. Notable works highlight his role as a lawyer and advocate for human rights, illustrating how his legal expertise supported SWAPO's efforts. The Civil Cooperation Bureau (CCB) is frequently discussed as a shadowy organization responsible for political assassinations during apartheid, including Lubowski's murder. Analysis of Lubowski's activism reveals his alignment with broader anti-apartheid movements across Southern Africa, emphasizing his commitment to non-violent resistance and political mobilization.

Anton Lubowski's contributions to the anti-apartheid movement were significant. He played a vital role in organizing protests and advocating for labor rights through his involvement with various unions. His philosophy centered on non-violent resistance and fostering dialogue between different racial groups. Key events included his participation in peace negotiations leading up to Namibia's independence and his efforts to raise awareness about human rights abuses.

Lubowski was assassinated outside his home on September 12th 1989, shortly before Namibia's first democratic elections. The CCB orchestrated this politically motivated killing to silence dissenting voices within the liberation movement. His assassination had profound implications for Namibia, highlighting the lengths to which the apartheid regime would go to maintain power and disrupt the transition to independence. The immediate aftermath of Lubowski's assassination galvanized support for SWAPO and intensified calls for justice in Namibia. His legacy endures as a symbol of resistance against oppression, influencing contemporary activists who continue to fight for social justice and equality. Memorials and commemorations honor his contributions, ensuring that his fight for human rights is not forgotten.

Khalil al-Wazir

Khalil al-Wazir, also known as Abu Jihad, is a significant figure in Palestinian history, recognized for his leadership in the Palestinian Liberation Organization (PLO) and his commitment to the Palestinian cause. Born on October 10th 1935, in Ramla, Palestine, al-Wazir's life was profoundly shaped by the events of the 1948 Arab-Israeli War, which resulted in the mass displacement of Palestinians and the establishment of the State of Israel. This conflict not only marked the beginning of al-Wazir's journey as a refugee but also set the stage for his lifelong activism against occupation and for Palestinian self-determination. The 1948 war led to the expulsion of thousands of Palestinians from their homes, creating a refugee crisis that continues to affect generations. Al-Wazir's experiences during this tumultuous period fueled his political awakening and commitment to armed struggle as a means to achieve liberation.

Khalil al-Wazir's family was expelled from their hometown of Ramla during the 1948 war when Zionist militias occupied the area. The family sought refuge in Gaza, where they faced the harsh realities of displacement alongside many other Palestinians. The refugee crisis in Palestine was characterized by loss, trauma, and a struggle for identity among displaced individuals. This environment profoundly influenced al-Wazir's perspective on resistance and national identity.

Growing up in Gaza, al-Wazir received an education facilitated by the United Nations Relief and Works Agency (UNRWA), which provided schooling for Palestinian refugees. His political awakening began during his university years in Cairo, where he met Yasir Arafat and became involved in anti-colonial activism. Influenced by pan-Arabism and socialist ideals, al-Wazir developed a commitment to armed struggle as a means to liberate Palestine from Israeli occupation. In 1958, he co-founded Fatah with Arafat and other young Palestinians, marking a pivotal moment in the Palestinian liberation movement. Fatah aimed to unite various factions under a single banner while promoting guerrilla warfare as a strategy against Israeli forces.

Al-Wazir quickly rose through the ranks of Fatah and subsequently became a key figure within the PLO after its establishment in 1964. As Deputy Commander in Chief of Palestinian forces, he was instrumental in planning military operations against Israeli targets and coordinating resistance activities across occupied territories. His leadership during significant events such as Black September in Jordan and the Israeli invasion of Lebanon in 1982 solidified his reputation as a military strategist. Al-Wazir also played a crucial role in fostering grassroots movements within Palestinian society, contributing to the emergence of youth committees that laid the groundwork for the First Intifada in 1987. His ability to balance military action with political diplomacy made him a respected leader among Palestinians.

On April 16th 1988, Khalil al-Wazir was assassinated by Israeli commandos during a raid on his home in Tunis. This operation was executed by Sayeret Matkal, an elite Israeli special forces unit, under orders from high ranking officials within Israel's government. Al-Wazir's assassination had immediate repercussions for Palestinian politics; it was perceived as an attempt to weaken the PLO leadership and disrupt ongoing resistance efforts. The assassination galvanized support for al-Wazir among Palestinians and reinforced their resolve against Israeli occupation. His death sparked protests across Palestinian territories and further intensified international attention on the plight of Palestinians.

Khalil al-Wazir's life and legacy continue to resonate within contemporary Palestinian identity and resistance movements. He is remembered not only as a military leader but also as a symbol of steadfastness against oppression. His contributions laid foundational elements for subsequent generations of activists who continue to fight for Palestinian rights.

Muhammad Sidi Brahim Sidi Embarek Basi

Muhammad Sidi Brahim Sidi Embarek Basir, a prominent Sahrawi nationalist leader, played a crucial role in the struggle for self-determination in Western Sahara during the late 1960s and early 1970s. Born in the early 1940s in the region that would later become known as Western Sahara, Basir emerged as a significant figure in the Sahrawi nationalist movement, advocating for the rights and independence of the Sahrawi people from colonial rule. His activism occurred during a critical period marked by the decline of Spanish colonialism and the rise of competing territorial claims from Morocco and Mauritania. The historical context of Western Sahara during the 1970s was characterized by a growing sense of national identity among Sahrawis, fueled by increasing political awareness and activism against colonial powers. The region's strategic importance, coupled with its rich natural resources, made it a focal point for both local and international political interests.

Muhammad Sidi Brahim Sidi Embarek Basir was born into a traditional Sahrawi family in the town of Smara. His early life was shaped by the socio-political dynamics of Western Sahara under Spanish colonial rule. Basir received his education in Spanish schools, where he became increasingly aware of the disparities faced by his people under colonial governance. In the late 1960s, as anti-colonial sentiments surged across

Africa, Basir became involved in nationalist movements advocating for Sahrawi rights. He was influenced by various factors, including exposure to pan-Arabism and socialist ideologies that emphasized liberation from colonial oppression. Key events that shaped his political ideology included witnessing protests against Spanish rule and participating in student organizations that promoted Sahrawi nationalism.

The Sahrawi nationalist movement gained momentum in the 1970s as various groups sought to unify efforts toward independence. Central to this movement was the Polisario Front, established in 1973 to fight for self-determination for the Sahrawi people. Basir's contributions to this movement were significant; he became a key figure within the organization, advocating for armed resistance against colonial forces. The goals of the Sahrawi nationalist movement included achieving independence from Spain and resisting Moroccan and Mauritanian territorial claims following Spain's withdrawal from Western Sahara. Major figures within the movement included Basir, alongside others like Yahya Bouhadi and Brahim Ghali, who collectively sought to galvanize support among Sahrawis and build international awareness of their plight.

On June 18th 1970, Muhammad Sidi Brahim Sidi Embarek Basir disappeared under mysterious circumstances following a demonstration known as the Zemla Intifada. This uprising marked a pivotal moment in Sahrawi history as it represented widespread discontent with Spanish colonial rule and called for greater autonomy for Western Sahara. The political climate at the time was tense; Spanish authorities responded harshly to any signs of dissent. Reports indicate that Basir was apprehended by members of the Spanish Legion during these protests. Eyewitness testimonies suggest that he was taken into custody but never seen again. Investigations into his disappearance have been complicated by a lack of transparency from Spanish authorities and ongoing political tensions surrounding Western Sahara.

Basir's disappearance had profound implications for the Sahrawi nationalist movement. It galvanized support among activists and highlighted the repressive measures employed by colonial powers against those advocating for independence. His fate remains emblematic of the broader struggles faced by Sahrawis seeking self-determination. In subsequent years, Basir's legacy has been honored within Sahrawi culture as a symbol of resistance against oppression. His contributions are remembered through commemorations and cultural narratives that emphasize his commitment to justice and national identity. The Polisario Front continues to invoke his memory in its ongoing struggle against Moroccan occupation.

Joe Nzingo Gqabi

Joe Nzingo Gqabi was a prominent figure in the struggle against apartheid in South Africa, born on April 6th 1929, in Aliwal North, Cape Province. Raised in an environment of oppression, he became politically active at a young age, joining the African National Congress (ANC) in 1952. His early life was marked by hardship; after moving to Johannesburg, he worked as a construction laborer while also pursuing journalism, which allowed him to expose the injustices of apartheid through the militant newspaper; New Age. The context of South Africa during the apartheid era was characterized by systemic racial segregation and oppression enforced by the National Party government from 1948 onwards. The ANC emerged as a pivotal organization advocating for the rights of black South Africans, seeking to dismantle apartheid and establish a democratic society.

The socio-political landscape of South Africa leading up to the 1980s was fraught with tension due to oppressive apartheid policies that marginalized black South Africans and other racial groups. The ANC's strategies evolved from peaceful protests to armed resistance with the formation of its military wing, Umkhonto we Sizwe (MK), in 1961. This shift was necessitated by the increasing brutality of the apartheid regime and its unwillingness to engage in meaningful dialogue. During this period, neighboring Zimbabwe (formerly Rhodesia) became a crucial base for ANC operations. Following Zimbabwe's independence in 1980, it served as a strategic hub for ANC activities aimed at supporting liberation efforts within South Africa.

Gqabi's political journey within the ANC was marked by resilience and leadership. After joining the ANC Youth League in 1950, he quickly rose through the ranks due to his dedication and activism. His involvement with MK began after he underwent military training abroad, which included time spent in China. Gqabi was arrested multiple times for his anti-apartheid activities, spending significant time on Robben Island alongside notable leaders like Nelson Mandela. By 1980, after Zimbabwe gained independence, Gqabi was appointed as the ANC's chief representative there. His role involved coordinating operations against apartheid and fostering relationships with Zimbabwean leaders. He played a vital part in various campaigns aimed at mobilizing support for the liberation struggle.

On July 31st 1981, Gqabi was assassinated at his home in Harare by operatives linked to the South African Defence Force. This event occurred amidst heightened tensions as apartheid forces sought to eliminate key figures in the anti-apartheid movement. Reports indicate that his assassination was part of a broader strategy to destabilize ANC operations abroad and intimidate exiled leaders.

The implications of Gqabi's assassination were profound; it not only represented a significant loss for the ANC but also galvanized support for the anti-apartheid struggle both locally and internationally. His death underscored the lengths to which the apartheid regime would go to maintain power and control. The immediate aftermath of Gqabi's assassination saw an intensification of anti-apartheid activities within South Africa and increased international condemnation of apartheid policies. His legacy is remembered as one of bravery and commitment to justice; he is celebrated not only within South Africa but also recognized globally as a martyr for freedom. Today, Gqabi is honored through various memorials and institutions named after him, reflecting his enduring impact on South African history and the fight for equality.

Waste Disposal In Northern Kenya

Oil exploration activities in Northern Kenya have gained momentum since significant discoveries were made in the Turkana region in 2012. Companies like Tullow Oil and Africa Oil have been at the forefront, drilling numerous wells and establishing infrastructure for oil extraction. While these activities promise economic growth and development, they also raise significant environmental concerns, particularly regarding waste disposal practices that may impact public health. Studying the environmental impacts of oil exploration is crucial as improper waste management can lead to serious health risks. Understanding these risks is vital for safeguarding community health and ensuring that economic benefits do not come at the expense of public well-being.

Oil exploration in Kenya began in earnest in the 1950s, with early efforts focused on the Lamu Basin. However, it wasn't until 2012 that substantial oil reserves were discovered in the Lokichar Basin, leading to increased interest from international oil companies. Tullow Oil's discovery of approximately 600 million barrels of oil equivalent marked a significant milestone in Kenya's oil history. The regulatory framework governing oil exploration and waste management in Kenya includes the Environmental Management and Coordination Act (EMCA) of 1999, which establishes guidelines for environmental protection and waste management.

The National Environment Management Authority (NEMA) oversees compliance with these regulations, but enforcement remains a challenge due to inadequate resources and capacity.

The typical processes involved in oil exploration include; Seismic Surveys by assessing geological formations to identify potential oil reserves, extracting core samples to determine the presence of hydrocarbons and extracting crude oil from identified reserves. These processes generate various types of waste which pose potential hazards to both environmental health and human health due to their toxic components.

Several oil exploration projects in Northern Kenya have raised concerns regarding waste disposal practices. In the Tullow Oil's Lokichar Project there was improper disposal of drilling mud and produced water, leading to soil and water contamination. Documented incidents of improper waste disposal have resulted in health impacts such as respiratory issues and skin diseases among local communities. A study highlighted increasing cases of upper respiratory tract infections linked to air pollution from nearby drilling activities.

Scientific literature has established a link between exposure to oil exploration waste and various health issues, including cancer. A systematic review found that petroleum industry workers face increased risks for lung cancer and leukemia due to exposure to hazardous materials used during extraction processes.

Statistical data from health surveys indicate rising cancer rates in Northern Kenya, correlating these trends with the expansion of oil exploration activities. The prevalence of cancers such as lung cancer has been notably higher in regions near active drilling sites compared to areas without such activities.

The socio-economic consequences for communities affected by poor waste management practices are profound. Local populations often face loss of livelihoods due to environmental degradation, increased healthcare costs associated with pollution related illnesses and social unrest stemming from inadequate government response to environmental concerns. Community responses have included activism against oil companies and calls for better health initiatives. Local organizations are working to raise awareness about health risks associated with oil exploration waste.

Radioactive Toxic Waste Shipment From Europe To Africa

The issue of radioactive toxic waste has emerged as a critical environmental health concern, particularly in developing regions like Africa. Between 1988 and 1994, significant shipments of radioactive toxic waste from Europe to the Somalia coast raised alarms regarding the implications for local communities and ecosystems. Greenpeace played a pivotal role in exposing these shipments, revealing that approximately 10 million tonnes of hazardous materials were involved.

During the late 20th century, European countries faced increasing challenges in managing hazardous waste due to stringent environmental regulations and growing public awareness. The disposal of toxic waste became a pressing issue, with many countries seeking cost effective solutions. Unfortunately, this led to unethical practices, including the export of hazardous waste to developing countries with lax environmental regulations. The motivations for shipping toxic waste to Africa were primarily economic and regulatory. European companies sought cheaper disposal options due to rising costs associated with domestic waste management. Additionally, developing nations often lacked the infrastructure and regulations necessary to handle hazardous waste safely, making them attractive targets for waste exporters.

The geopolitical landscape in Somalia during this period was characterized by instability and civil unrest, which created a vacuum that allowed illegal activities, including toxic waste dumping, to proliferate. The collapse of central authority made it easier for foreign entities to exploit local vulnerabilities.

Greenpeace employed various investigative methods to uncover the shipments of radioactive toxic waste. Conducting on site assessments at suspected dumping locations along the Somalia coast, gathering statistics on reported shipments and analyzing shipping records and engaging with local communities and stakeholders to document their experiences and observations related to toxic waste dumping. These methods helped Greenpeace compile evidence that highlighted the scale and impact of the issue. Between 1988 and 1994, over 10 million tonnes of hazardous waste were shipped from Europe to Africa; radioactive materials containing isotopes such as cesium-137 and strontium-90 and chemical waste including heavy metals and industrial byproducts.

Specific locations along the Somalia coast that were impacted were Eel Ma'aan which is a port area where evidence suggested containers filled with toxic waste were buried and Mogadishu where reports indicated that waste was dumped in coastal areas near urban settlements. The short term environmental impacts included soil contamination and water pollution, while long term effects manifested as biodiversity loss and degradation of marine ecosystems. Local communities reported increased health issues linked to exposure to these toxic materials.

Communities experienced health crises, including increased rates of cancer and other diseases attributed to exposure. The fishing industry suffered due to contaminated waters, leading to loss of livelihoods for local fishermen.

Tom Mboya

Tom Mboya was a prominent figure in Kenya's political landscape, known for his significant contributions to the country's independence and development. Born on August 15th 1930, he emerged as a key leader in the Kenya African National Union (KANU) and served as the Minister for Economic Planning and Development until his assassination on July 5th 1969. Mboya was instrumental in negotiating Kenya's independence from British colonial rule and was a champion of Pan-Africanism, advocating for the liberation of African nations and the empowerment of their people. The late 1960s in Kenya were marked by political tension, ethnic divisions, and the struggle for power within KANU. President Jomo Kenyatta's government faced challenges from various factions, including radical elements within the party that sought more socialist policies. Mboya's assassination occurred against this backdrop of political strife and growing unrest, leading to significant implications for Kenyan society and governance.

On July 5th 1969, Tom Mboya was gunned down shortly after leaving Chaani's Pharmacy on Government Road (now Moi Avenue) in Nairobi. Witnesses reported that he was shot at point blank range by Nahashon Isaac Njenga Njoroge as he exited the pharmacy. The shooting occurred around 1:30 PM, just moments before Mboya was set to attend a football match between his favorite teams.

The location of the incident was significant; it was a busy area in Nairobi's central business district. Mboya had been unaccompanied by his usual security detail, which raised questions about his safety and the circumstances leading to his assassination. Eyewitness accounts described chaos following the shooting, with crowds gathering as police arrived to control the situation. Mboya was rushed to Nairobi Hospital but succumbed to his injuries shortly after arrival.

Nahashon Isaac Njenga Njoroge was quickly identified as Mboya's assassin. Njenga had previously been part of a military training program in Bulgaria, which Mboya had facilitated as part of an initiative to empower Kenyan youth. His motivations for killing Mboya remain unclear but are often speculated to be politically motivated or rooted in personal grievances. Njenga's trial began on August 19th 1969. The prosecution presented evidence linking him to the murder weapon and eyewitness testimonies that placed him at the scene. During the trial, Njenga made a controversial statement; "Why don't you go after the big man?" This remark has fueled speculation about whether there were larger political forces behind Mboya's assassination.

Despite the evidence against him, questions about the integrity of the trial process and potential political interference lingered. Ultimately, Njenga was convicted and sentenced to death by hanging;

however, details surrounding his execution were shrouded in secrecy.

Mboya's assassination had immediate and far reaching political implications in Kenya. Many viewed it as a politically motivated killing orchestrated by factions within KANU who opposed his progressive policies and influence. Following his death, widespread riots erupted across Kenya, particularly in Nyanza Province, where Mboya enjoyed considerable support. Political figures responded with shock and outrage; however, there were also accusations that Kenyatta's government might have benefited from eliminating a rival who posed a threat to their power dynamics. The public outcry following Mboya's death highlighted deep seated frustrations with government repression and ethnic favoritism within political structures. The aftermath of Mboya's assassination marked a turning point in Kenyan politics. It solidified Kenyatta's grip on power while simultaneously stifling dissenting voices within KANU. The event is often cited as a catalyst for increased political repression in Kenya during subsequent years.

Tom Mboya is remembered as one of Kenya's founding fathers whose vision for an equitable society shaped early post-independence policies. His contributions included advocating for education reforms and economic planning that aimed to uplift marginalized communities.

The legacy of his assassination continues to resonate in contemporary Kenyan politics. It underscored the dangers faced by political leaders advocating for reform within an increasingly authoritarian regime. The subsequent rise of ethnic politics and factionalism within KANU can be traced back to this pivotal moment in history.

Hamza Al Dahdouh

Hamza Al Dahdouh was a prominent journalist working for Al Quds TV who was killed on October 15th 2023, during an airstrike in Khan Younis while covering ongoing military operations. Al Dahdouh was reportedly traveling in a vehicle marked as "Press" when it was struck by an Israeli missile. This incident occurred amidst a broader military campaign by Israel. Eyewitness accounts indicate that despite being clearly identifiable as a journalist, the attack appeared deliberate. The killing of Hamza Al Dahdouh raises significant concerns regarding press freedom in conflict zones. It exemplifies a troubling trend where journalists are increasingly targeted. Such targeted killings can deter journalists from reporting on critical issues, leading to self-censorship. Attacks on journalists violate international laws that protect civilians during armed conflicts. The UN has condemned these actions as potential war crimes.

Targeting journalists undermines the ability of media organizations to report accurately from conflict zones. This results in a lack of comprehensive coverage that informs both local and international audiences about the realities on the ground and increased propaganda as narratives may be shaped by unverified sources without journalistic oversight. Journalists face both psychological trauma from witnessing violence and physical risks from direct attacks. Many experience PTSD or other mental health issues due to their exposure to conflict related trauma.

Mustafa Thuraya

Mustafa Thuraya was a journalist working for Al Quds TV who was killed on October 15th 2023, during an airstrike in Khan Younis. Thuraya was reportedly covering an airstrike when he was killed. Eyewitnesses indicated that he was clearly identifiable as a journalist at the time of the attack.

Reports indicate that at least five journalists were specifically targeted by Israeli forces during this period. Such actions not only violate international humanitarian law but also contribute to a hostile environment for media personnel.

The targeted killings of journalists like Mustafa Thuraya reveal critical vulnerabilities within conflict reporting frameworks. These incidents not only threaten individual lives but also undermine press freedom and accountability mechanisms essential for democratic societies.

Ghassan Najjar

Ghassan Najjar was a journalist who tragically lost his life while covering military actions in Gaza. His case exemplifies the dangers faced by media professionals in conflict zones. Ghassan Najjar was known for his dedication to reporting on the humanitarian situation in Gaza. He worked for local media outlets and had built a reputation for his commitment to uncovering the truth behind the ongoing conflict.

On November 1st 2023, Najjar was injured by shrapnel during an Israeli airstrike while reporting on military actions in Khan Younis. Eyewitness accounts describe how he was clearly identifiable as a journalist at the time of the incident.

Following Najjar's death, various media organizations condemned the incident. Reporters Without Borders and other advocacy groups called for accountability regarding attacks on journalists. Colleagues expressed their grief and outrage over the loss of a fellow journalist dedicated to informing the public about critical issues.

Wissam Kassem

Wissam Kassem was a cameraman for Al-Manar TV who tragically lost his life while covering military actions in Gaza City.

On November 1st 2023, Kassem was killed during an Israeli airstrike that targeted journalists. Eyewitness accounts indicate that he was clearly identified as a journalist at the time of the attack. Reports suggest that he was filming military operations when shrapnel from the airstrike struck him fatally.

Following Kassem's death, various media organizations condemned the incident. Reporters Without Borders and other advocacy groups called for accountability regarding attacks on journalists. Colleagues expressed their grief and outrage over the loss of a dedicated journalist committed to informing the public about critical issues.

International humanitarian law provides protections for journalists operating in conflict zones. According to Article 79 of Additional Protocol I to the Geneva Conventions, journalists engaged in dangerous missions should be treated as civilians under international law. Targeting journalists violates these principles and can constitute a war crime.

Lev Tahor

Lev Tahor, which translates to "Pure Heart" in Hebrew, is an ultra-Orthodox Jewish sect founded in 1988 by Shlomo Helbrans in Israel. The group is often described as a cult and has been the subject of numerous controversies, including allegations of child abuse, forced marriages, and human trafficking. Over the years, Lev Tahor has relocated multiple times, seeking refuge from legal scrutiny in various countries, including the United States, Canada, Mexico, and most recently Guatemala. Lev Tahor emerged from a strict interpretation of Jewish law, promoting a lifestyle that includes rigorous religious observance and separation from mainstream society. The sect has faced numerous allegations over the years, including accusations of child abuse, forced marriages of minors to much older men, and psychological manipulation.

In various countries where Lev Tahor has settled, legal issues have arisen. In Canada, for instance, authorities investigated claims of child neglect and abuse in 2013. Legal actions led to children being removed from their families due to concerns about their welfare. Guatemala's legal framework regarding human trafficking and child protection is relatively robust; however, enforcement can be challenging due to limited resources and coordination among agencies.

On December 20th 2024, Guatemalan authorities conducted a significant raid on Lev Tahor's compound located in Oratorio city. The operation involved approximately 480 police officers and military personnel who responded to complaints about widespread abuse within the community. During this raid, officials rescued at least 160 minors and 40 women from potentially abusive conditions. Reports indicate that investigators discovered evidence suggesting human trafficking practices within Lev Tahor, including forced marriages and systemic abuse. Prosecutors have stated that they found suspected remains of minors buried on the premises, further raising alarm about possible fatalities linked to the sect's practices. Officials emphasized that protecting children is a top priority as investigations continue.

The allegations surrounding Lev Tahor include serious accusations related to human trafficking. Evidence presented during the raid indicates that minors were subjected to forced marriages and other forms of exploitation. The potential impact on victims is profound; many may face long term psychological trauma due to their experiences within the sect. The legal ramifications for Lev Tahor following this raid could be extensive. Charges related to human trafficking, mistreatment of minors, and other crimes are being considered against members of the sect. This situation raises critical questions about balancing religious freedom with child protection rights.

Eric DeValkenaere

On December 3rd 2019, Eric DeValkenaere, a former police officer in Kansas City, Missouri, fatally shot Cameron Lamb, a 26 year old Black man, while responding to a reported traffic incident. The shooting occurred as Lamb was backing his pickup truck into his garage. DeValkenaere and another officer, Detective Troy Schwalm, approached the vehicle without a warrant or probable cause, leading to a tragic confrontation that ended with Lamb's death. This case has garnered significant attention due to its implications for police use of force, racial dynamics in law enforcement, and the broader societal discourse surrounding justice and accountability in America.

The legal proceedings against DeValkenaere began with his indictment on charges of involuntary manslaughter and armed criminal action. The prosecution argued that DeValkenaere acted recklessly by entering Lamb's property without consent or a warrant and shooting him within seconds of arrival. The trial revealed that Lamb was unarmed at the time of the shooting; a gun found at the scene was later disputed by Lamb's family as having been planted.

In November 2021, DeValkenaere was convicted of second degree involuntary manslaughter and armed criminal action. The court emphasized that he had violated Lamb's constitutional rights by entering the property illegally and using deadly force against an unarmed individual. The conviction carried significant implications for police accountability, highlighting the legal standards governing the use of force by law enforcement officers.

On December 20th 2024, Missouri Governor Mike Parson commuted DeValkenaere's sentence after he had served just over a year in prison. This decision sparked outrage among community members and civil rights advocates who viewed it as an affront to justice for Lamb's family. Parson justified his decision by stating that he had carefully considered various clemency petitions but faced criticism for not consulting with Lamb's family or community leaders prior to making his decision. Public statements from officials like Jackson County Prosecutor Jean Peters Baker reflected deep concern over the message this commutation sent regarding accountability for police officers involved in fatal shootings. Baker noted that "DeValkenaere was convicted for killing an unarmed man" and criticized the governor for showing "incredible mercy" to the former officer while failing to extend similar compassion to the victim's family.

The Kansas City community reacted strongly to both DeValkenaere's conviction and subsequent commutation. Civil rights organizations organized protests demanding justice for Cameron Lamb and accountability for police violence. Advocacy groups highlighted systemic issues within law enforcement regarding racial bias and excessive use of force.

Comparing DeValkenaere's case to other incidents involving police use of deadly force reveals significant patterns regarding racial dynamics and legal outcomes. Cases such as those involving Derek Chauvin (George Floyd) or Michael Slager (Walter Scott) highlight similar themes of accountability or lack thereof when officers are involved in fatal encounters with Black individuals.

The Execution of Marcellus Williams

Marcellus Williams was convicted in 2001 for the 1998 murder of Felicia Gayle, a journalist found stabbed in her home in a suburb of St. Louis, Missouri. Despite maintaining his innocence throughout his time on death row, Williams faced execution on September 24th 2024, after Governor Mike Parson declined to halt the process. This decision has significant implications for the discourse surrounding capital punishment, particularly concerning issues of potential innocence and ethical governance in the justice system. Governor Parson's role in this case highlights the intersection of legal authority and moral responsibility in capital punishment cases.

The legal framework for capital punishment in Missouri is governed by state law, which outlines the procedures for sentencing and executing individuals convicted of murder. Missouri has seen a trend toward more rigorous scrutiny of death penalty cases, especially regarding claims of innocence and procedural fairness. The case of Marcellus Williams is emblematic of these concerns. Williams' conviction was marred by allegations of racial bias during jury selection, ineffective legal representation, and the mishandling of DNA evidence. In 2016, DNA testing revealed that the male DNA found on the murder weapon did not match Williams, raising substantial questions about his guilt. Despite these findings, multiple attempts to vacate his conviction were unsuccessful until his execution date was set.

Governor Parson's decision to proceed with Williams' execution despite significant public opposition and calls for clemency reflects complex political and social dynamics. In his statement, Parson emphasized adherence to the law and faith in the judicial system's integrity, asserting that Williams had exhausted all legal avenues to prove his innocence. However, this stance has been criticized as neglecting the moral implications of executing a potentially innocent man. Political pressures may have influenced Parson's decision; as a Republican governor, he may have felt compelled to align with party constituents who support capital punishment as a deterrent to crime. Additionally, social factors such as public opinion regarding crime and punishment in Missouri likely played a role in shaping his response to clemency requests.

The implications of Governor Parson's decision are profound for various stakeholders. For Marcellus Williams, the execution represents a tragic culmination of years spent fighting for justice and exoneration. For victims' families, including those of Felicia Gayle, there is a complex emotional landscape; while some may feel closure through the execution, others have publicly opposed it, advocating instead for life imprisonment without parole. The role of the U.S. Supreme Court also comes into play; their refusal to intervene at the last minute underscores broader issues related to capital punishment in America. The

Court's decisions often set precedents that influence future cases involving similar claims of innocence or procedural errors. Public opinion regarding capital punishment remains divided, with many advocating for its abolition due to concerns about wrongful convictions and racial disparities within the justice system. In Williams' case, significant advocacy efforts emerged from civil rights organizations that highlighted potential flaws in his trial and raised alarms about executing an innocent person.

Ethical considerations surrounding this case are paramount; executing individuals without incontrovertible evidence of guilt raises serious moral questions about state sanctioned death penalties. State officials have a responsibility to ensure that justice is served fairly and equitably, an obligation that becomes increasingly critical when potential innocence is at stake.

Yasser al-Zahrani

Yasser al-Zahrani was captured in Afghanistan in late 2001 at the age of 17. He was reportedly apprehended while attempting to flee the conflict. Following his capture, al-Zahrani was transferred to Guantanamo Bay, where he was classified as an "enemy combatant." The circumstances surrounding his capture and subsequent detention raise questions about the legality and ethics of U.S. actions during this period.

The early 2000s were marked by heightened security concerns following the September 11th attacks in 2001. The U.S. government adopted aggressive counterterrorism measures, leading to the establishment of policies that allowed for extrajudicial detentions. This geopolitical climate fostered an environment where individuals could be detained without due process, significantly impacting U.S. detention policies. Conditions at Guantanamo Bay have been widely criticized for their harshness and lack of transparency. Detainees faced solitary confinement, limited access to legal representation, and inadequate medical care. Reports indicate that many detainees were subjected to torture and inhumane treatment, raising serious human rights concerns.

During his time at Guantanamo, al-Zahrani faced a legal limbo characterized by a lack of formal charges and due process. The Military Commissions Act of 2006 further complicated matters by limiting detainees' rights to challenge their detention in court. Al-Zahrani's case exemplifies the challenges faced by many detainees who were denied basic legal protections. In early 2006, U.S. authorities decided to clear al-Zahrani of all charges, citing insufficient evidence to justify his continued detention. This decision came amid growing scrutiny over the treatment of detainees at Guantanamo and increasing pressure from human rights organizations advocating for accountability.

Following his release in April 2006, Yasser al-Zahrani returned to home but faced significant challenges reintegrating into society after years of detention. He struggled with the psychological impacts of his experience, including anxiety and social isolation. The psychological effects of wrongful detention can be profound and long-lasting. Many former detainees report symptoms consistent with PTSD, difficulty adjusting to civilian life, and strained relationships with family and friends due to their experiences during incarceration.

Al-Zahrani's story fits within a larger narrative concerning Guantanamo Bay detainees who were subjected to similar injustices. The facility has become a symbol of human rights violations associated with counterterrorism efforts, prompting calls for reform from various human rights organizations.

Abdul Razak Ali Yemen

Abdul Razak Ali Yemen is one of the many individuals who became a victim of the Guantanamo Bay controversial detention system. Captured in 2002, Yemen was held at Guantanamo for five years before being released without charges, having been found innocent of any wrongdoing. His case highlights not only the personal ramifications of indefinite detention but also broader issues regarding justice and human rights in the context of U.S. counterterrorism policies.

Abdul Razak Ali Yemen was captured in Pakistan in 2002 amidst a broader geopolitical climate characterized by heightened tensions following the U.S.-led invasion of Afghanistan. The invasion aimed to dismantle Al-Qaeda and remove the Taliban from power, resulting in widespread military operations that often led to the capture of individuals based on limited intelligence or suspicion rather than concrete evidence. Yemen's capture was influenced by these geopolitical dynamics, as many detainees were apprehended under dubious circumstances during chaotic military engagements. The legal framework governing detention at Guantanamo has been heavily criticized for its lack of transparency and adherence to international human rights standards. The U.S. government asserted that detainees were not entitled to the protections typically afforded under both U.S. law and the Geneva Conventions because they were classified as "enemy combatants." This classification allowed for indefinite detention without charge or trial, raising significant ethical and legal concerns regarding due process and human rights violations.

During his five years at Guantanamo, Abdul Razak Ali Yemen experienced harsh conditions and treatment that have been widely reported by human rights organizations. Detainees at Guantanamo have reported instances of torture, including physical abuse, psychological manipulation, and inadequate medical care. Yemen's treatment exemplifies the broader allegations against the facility, which has been described as a site where detainees are subjected to inhumane conditions that violate both domestic and international standards. Reports from various human rights groups indicate that many detainees were held in solitary confinement, denied access to legal representation, and subjected to "enhanced interrogation techniques" that many experts classify as torture. Such practices have drawn widespread condemnation from international bodies and civil rights organizations.

The legal proceedings surrounding Abdul Razak Ali Yemen's detention were fraught with challenges and inconsistencies. Initially captured under dubious circumstances, Yemen faced significant obstacles in contesting his detention due to the lack of formal charges against him. The evidence presented during his time in detention was often based on unreliable intelligence or coerced testimonies. The military commissions set up to try detainees at Guantanamo have been criticized for lacking fairness and transparency. Many detainees were unable to mount an effective defense due to restrictions on evidence disclosure and limited access to legal counsel. Ultimately, after years of captivity without trial or formal charges, Yemen was released in 2007 when it was determined that he posed no threat to U.S. national security.

Abdul Razak Ali Yemen's release came after extensive advocacy from human rights organizations that highlighted his wrongful detention. Upon his release, he faced significant challenges reintegrating into society after years of imprisonment without trial. The psychological impact of his detention has reportedly left lasting scars, complicating his ability to rebuild his life.

Essam al-Rimi

Essam al-Rimi, a Yemeni national, was detained at Guantanamo Bay from 2002 until his release in September 2007. His case is emblematic of the broader issues surrounding the detention policies at Guantanamo, including the lack of transparency and the implications for human rights. Al-Rimi's background as a Yemeni citizen caught in the geopolitical turmoil following the September 11th attacks provides critical context for understanding his detention and subsequent release.

Essam al-Rimi was captured in 2002 during a U.S.-led operation in Afghanistan. The U.S. government claimed that he was affiliated with Al-Qaeda and had participated in hostilities against U.S. forces. Following his capture, al-Rimi was transferred to Guantanamo Bay, where he became one of many detainees subjected to indefinite detention. Initial assessments by U.S. authorities deemed him a security threat based on limited intelligence. In 2004 Al-Rimi's case began to draw attention as legal challenges to Guantanamo's detention practices grew. By 2007, after years of legal battles and advocacy from human rights organizations, al-Rimi was cleared for release.

The reasons given by the U.S. government for al-Rimi's capture included allegations of involvement with terrorist organizations; however, these claims were often based on unreliable intelligence sources. The legal proceedings surrounding Essam al-Rimi's case were complex and fraught with challenges.

Initially classified as an enemy combatant, he faced significant hurdles in contesting his detention due to the lack of formal charges against him.

Al-Rimi's legal team filed habeas corpus petitions challenging the legality of his detention. In landmark cases such as Rasul v. Bush (2004), the Supreme Court ruled that detainees had the right to challenge their detention in U.S. courts, which opened avenues for legal representation and review. His defense argued that the evidence against him was insufficient and based on coerced testimonies or unreliable intelligence. Despite being held for years without formal charges, al-Rimi's eventual release came after it was determined that he posed no threat to national security.

Ali Abdul Aziz Ali

Ali Abdul Aziz Ali, also known as Ammar al-Baluchi, is a Pakistani national who was detained at Guantanamo Bay from 2006 until his release in May 2013. His case is significant not only because of the allegations against him but also due to the broader implications for international law and human rights, particularly concerning the treatment of detainees and the legal processes surrounding their detention.

Ali Abdul Aziz Ali was arrested in April 2003 in Karachi, Pakistan. He was initially held in a secret CIA detention facility where he reportedly endured extensive torture before being transferred to Guantanamo Bay on September 6th 2006. The U.S. government accused him of various charges related to terrorism, including conspiracy and providing material support to the September 11th hijackers.

Ali Abdul Aziz Ali's treatment included physical abuse and psychological manipulation, consistent with reports from other detainees regarding their experiences at the facility. He was held for years without formal charges being brought against him until military commissions were established to try cases related to terrorism. He faced numerous legal challenges during his time at Guantanamo Bay. Initially classified as an enemy combatant, he was subjected to military commissions rather than traditional court proceedings.

The U.S. established military commissions to try detainees accused of terrorism related offenses after the Supreme Court ruled against earlier commission structures in Hamdan v. Rumsfeld (2006). Despite this, proceedings against Ali were delayed for years due to various legal and procedural issues. His defense team argued that the evidence against him was obtained through torture and was therefore inadmissible. Furthermore, they contended that holding him without formal charges violated both U.S. law and international human rights norms. The broader implications of his case highlight systemic issues within the military commission system and raise concerns about the fairness of trials for detainees at Guantanamo Bay.

Ali Abdul Aziz Ali's eventual release in May 2013 came after years of legal battles and advocacy from human rights organizations that highlighted his wrongful detention. Investigations revealed that many allegations against him were based on coerced confessions and unreliable intelligence. His release contributed to growing public scrutiny regarding the legality and morality of holding individuals indefinitely without trial at Guantanamo Bay.

Pylos Shipwreck In June 2023

On June 14th 2023, a tragic shipwreck occurred off the coast of Pylos, Greece, when a fishing trawler named Adriana sank while carrying an estimated 750 migrants. This incident is one of the deadliest maritime disasters in recent history, with over 600 people presumed dead. The Adriana, which had departed from Tobruk, Libya, was en route to Italy when it capsized in international waters. The Mediterranean region has a long history of migration, shaped by socio-political factors and economic conditions. The area serves as a critical route for migrants fleeing conflict, persecution, and poverty in their home countries.

The journey to Pylos often involves perilous sea routes from North Africa, particularly Libya. Statistics indicate that thousands attempt this crossing annually, with many risking their lives on overcrowded vessels. Ongoing conflicts in countries such as Syria and Afghanistan, coupled with economic instability in regions like sub-Saharan Africa, have driven many to seek refuge in Europe. Additionally, restrictive border policies and a lack of safe pathways for migration exacerbate these issues.

On June 10th 2023, the Adriana set sail from Tobruk. By June 13th, distress signals were sent out as the vessel became increasingly unstable due to overcrowding. Despite being aware of the situation, Greek authorities delayed intervention. The Adriana was a fishing trawler with a maximum capacity of around 400 people but was carrying approximately 750 at the time of sinking. Reports indicated that many passengers were locked below deck during the incident. Contrary to initial claims that weather conditions contributed to the disaster, reports indicate that conditions were calm prior to the sinking.

The majority of migrants were from Pakistan, Syria, Palestine, and Egypt. Many were fleeing dire circumstances in their home countries. Of the estimated 750 individuals aboard, only 104 survived. The psychological and physical toll on survivors is significant, with many experiencing trauma from their ordeal.

Current Mediterranean migration policies often prioritize border control over humanitarian assistance. This incident highlights failures in search and rescue operations that need urgent reform.

Ahmed Abba

Journalists play a crucial role in conflict zones by providing vital information that can influence public opinion, inform policy decisions, and promote accountability. Their work often involves exposing human rights abuses, corruption, and the complexities of warfare, which can put them at significant risk. Ahmed Abba was a prominent journalist for Radio France Internationale (RFI), particularly known for his reporting on Boko Haram's activities in Cameroon. His abduction and subsequent murder by Boko Haram on July 30th 2015, underscore the extreme dangers faced by journalists in conflict areas and highlight the broader implications for press freedom and safety.

Cameroon has been grappling with a complex socio-political landscape, particularly in its Far North region, where Boko Haram has established a stronghold since 2014. The group exploits local grievances and socio-economic vulnerabilities to recruit members and conduct violent attacks. Globally, journalists in conflict zones face numerous threats, including violence, censorship, and legal repercussions. In Africa, these dangers are exacerbated by political instability and authoritarian regimes that often target media personnel to suppress dissent and control narratives.

Abba's investigative journalism focused on the intersection of corruption and terrorism, particularly how local governance failures contributed to the rise of Boko Haram. His reports shed light on the plight of refugees and the socio-economic conditions that allowed the group to flourish. Notable stories included detailed accounts of Boko Haram's recruitment strategies and their impact on local communities.

On July 30th 2015, Abba was abducted by Boko Haram after attending a meeting with local officials in Maroua. Following his kidnapping, he was held captive for several days before being executed. His murder sent shockwaves through the journalistic community and raised alarms about the safety of reporters operating in conflict zones like Cameroon.

Martinez Zogo

Martinez Zogo, a prominent Cameroonian journalist and director of Amplitude FM, was known for his fearless investigative reporting on corruption and governance issues. His work often targeted high profile figures, including media moguls and government officials, making him a significant voice in the fight against corruption in Cameroon. Tragically, Zogo was abducted on January 17th 2023, and his mutilated body was discovered five days later, on January 22nd 2023. His murder not only shocked the nation but also highlighted the severe risks journalists face in Cameroon, particularly when confronting powerful interests.

The media landscape in Cameroon is characterized by a high number of outlets; over 600 newspapers, nearly 200 radio stations, and more than 60 television channels. However, this diversity masks a troubling reality; journalists often operate under oppressive conditions marked by censorship, intimidation, and violence. Journalists in Cameroon face significant challenges, especially those investigating corruption. The country has been ranked among the worst for press freedom in Africa, with many journalists experiencing threats and violence for their work. The environment is particularly perilous for those like Zogo who expose corruption involving influential figures. The lack of legal protections and the prevalence of self-censorship further complicate the situation for media professionals in the country.

On January 17th 2023, Martinez Zogo was last seen leaving Amplitude FM after finishing his radio show "Embouteillage," where he often discussed corruption and governance issues. Reports indicate that he had received threats related to his investigations into corrupt practices involving prominent individuals, including media mogul Jean Pierre Amougou Belinga. Zogo's abduction involved unidentified assailants who forcibly took him from his vehicle near a police station in Yaounde. His body was discovered on January 22nd in Soa, a suburb of Yaounde, showing signs of severe torture, his fingers were severed, and he had suffered multiple injuries consistent with electric shocks and other brutal treatment. The gruesome nature of his death raised alarm bells about the safety of journalists in Cameroon.

The murder of Martinez Zogo elicited widespread condemnation both nationally and internationally. Journalists' associations and human rights organizations swiftly condemned the act as an attack on press freedom. The Syndicat National des Journalistes du Cameroun (SNJC) organized protests where journalists wore black to mourn Zogo's death and demand justice. Public outcry was significant; close to one hundred journalists met with the Minister of Communication to express their outrage over the killing. Human Rights Watch and other organizations called for an independent investigation into Zogo's murder, emphasizing that such acts of violence send chilling messages to other journalists working in similar environments.

Regina Martinez Perez

Regina Martinez Perez was a dedicated Mexican journalist known for her incisive reporting on drug related violence and corruption, particularly in the state of Veracruz. As a correspondent for the national magazine Proceso, she focused on the intricate connections between organized crime and government officials, making her work both significant and perilous. Martinez's murder on April 28th 2012, marked a tragic turning point for press freedom in Mexico, illustrating the severe risks faced by journalists in a country plagued by violence and impunity. Before Martinez's murder, the state of journalism in Mexico was already fraught with challenges. Journalists faced threats from organized crime, government censorship, and a culture of impunity that discouraged reporting on corruption and violence. According to reports, at least 164 journalists have been killed in Mexico since 1997, with Veracruz being one of the deadliest states for the press.

The environment of drug violence and corruption significantly impacted journalists' ability to report freely. By 2012, Mexico was recognized as one of the most dangerous countries for journalists globally. Statistics indicate that between 2000 and 2014 alone, at least 110 journalists were murdered or disappeared due to their work. The pervasive influence of drug cartels created an atmosphere where reporting on criminal activities often resulted in threats or violent reprisals against journalists.

Regina Martinez Perez was found dead in her home in Xalapa, Veracruz, on April 28th 2012. Her body showed signs of brutal assault, including asphyxia and physical injuries consistent with strangulation and beatings. Prior to her death, Martinez had reported extensively on issues related to drug cartels, including the arrest of high ranking cartel members and police corruption linked to organized crime. The investigation into her murder was marred by serious irregularities. Authorities arrested Jorge Antonio Hernández Silva, who was convicted based on a confession obtained under torture; however, many colleagues and human rights advocates believe that Martinez was targeted specifically for her investigative work rather than being a victim of a robbery gone wrong.

The immediate reactions to Martinez's murder were profound. Media organizations both nationally and internationally condemned the killing as an attack on press freedom. Human rights organizations called for thorough investigations into her death, emphasizing the need for accountability in a country where violence against journalists is rampant. National media coverage highlighted the growing crisis of journalist safety in Mexico, with many outlets using Martinez's story to illustrate the dangers reporters face when covering drug related issues.

John Williams Ntwali

The context of journalism in Rwanda is complex, shaped by a history of repression and state control. Following the 1994 genocide, the Rwandan government has maintained tight control over the media, often stifling dissenting voices. John Williams Ntwali, an investigative journalist and editor of The Chronicles, emerged as a significant figure in this landscape, known for his critical reporting on governance, human rights violations, and corruption. His tragic death on January 18th 2023, under suspicious circumstances, underscores the urgent need for enhanced protections for journalists in Rwanda.

Historically, press freedom in Rwanda has been severely restricted. The government has employed various tactics to suppress dissenting voices, including censorship, intimidation, and violence against journalists. The Rwandan media landscape is characterized by a lack of independent outlets and a pervasive culture of fear among journalists. Ntwali's work often highlighted issues of government corruption and human rights abuses, making him a target for retribution. Prior to his death, he reported on sensitive topics such as the imprisonment of political opponents and allegations of torture against detainees. His investigations not only exposed systemic corruption but also illustrated the risks faced by those who dare to challenge the status quo. Previous incidents of attacks against journalists in

Rwanda further illustrate this perilous environment. For example, several journalists have faced harassment or imprisonment for their reporting on government activities or human rights violations, creating a chilling effect on investigative journalism.

On January 18th 2023, John Williams Ntwali was reported dead following a traffic incident in Kigali. Official accounts state that he was a passenger on a motorcycle taxi when it was struck by a vehicle at approximately 2:50 AM. However, discrepancies between police claims and eyewitness accounts have raised suspicions regarding the true nature of his death. Eyewitnesses reported that Ntwali had expressed concerns about being followed and threatened prior to the incident. Friends noted that he had survived previous "staged accidents," indicating a pattern of intimidation linked to his journalistic work. The police's swift conclusion that it was merely an accident has been met with skepticism by media organizations and human rights advocates who demand an independent investigation into the circumstances surrounding his death.

The immediate reaction to Ntwali's death was one of shock and outrage among media organizations, civil society groups, and the public. Many viewed his murder as an attack on press freedom and a stark reminder of the dangers faced by journalists in Rwanda.

Rebel Groups In The Democratic Republic of Congo

The Democratic Republic of Congo (DRC) has been embroiled in conflict since its independence from Belgium, primarily driven by a complex interplay of political instability, ethnic tensions, and competition for vast mineral resources. Following the Rwandan Genocide in 1994, the DRC became a battleground for various armed groups, many of which were backed by neighboring countries seeking to exploit the DRC's rich deposits of precious stones and raw materials, such as gold and diamonds. The conflict has led to widespread human rights abuses and has resulted in millions of deaths, making it one of the deadliest conflicts since World War II. The significance of these resources cannot be overstated; they have fueled both local and international interests, leading to a protracted cycle of violence and exploitation.

Rebel groups in the DRC have relied heavily on external financing to sustain their operations. This funding comes from various sources, including individuals, foreign governments, and multinational corporations. Notable figures include leaders from Rwanda and Uganda who have been accused of providing military and financial support to groups like the M23 (March 23 Movement). Reports suggest that these governments have strategic interests in maintaining influence over eastern DRC, particularly due to its mineral wealth. The motivations behind this support often include economic gain from resource extraction and political leverage over the DRC government. For instance, during the M23's rise in 2012, there were allegations that Rwandan officials were directly involved in funding and supplying arms to the group. A significant case is the involvement of Uganda's military during its occupation of northeastern Congo from 1998 to 2003. Ugandan forces reportedly extracted gold worth millions while supporting local militias. Moreover, a UN panel has documented how these armed groups engage in illegal mining operations that fund their military activities.

Several African presidents have played pivotal roles in financing or supporting rebel factions within the DRC. Paul Kagame's (Rwanda) government has been implicated in backing various rebel groups, including the M23. His administration's support is often framed as a response to security concerns regarding Rwandan Hutu militants based in eastern DRC. Yoweri Museveni's (Uganda) regime has also been accused of providing support to Congolese rebels for both economic and strategic reasons. Uganda's involvement has been linked to securing control over lucrative mining regions. Evidence suggests that transactions between these governments and rebel groups often involve arms deals or resource sharing agreements that benefit both parties at the expense of local populations.

The financing of rebel groups by external actors has profound implications for local communities. The presence of armed groups has led to increased violence against civilians, including displacement and human rights abuses. Communities often find themselves caught between rival factions fighting for control over resources. Local economies suffer as conflict disrupts agricultural activities and trade. The exploitation of resources by armed groups diverts wealth away from local populations, exacerbating poverty. The ongoing conflict undermines governance structures within the DRC. Local leaders may align with different factions based on external support, further fragmenting political unity.

The international community has responded with varying degrees of engagement. The UN Security Council has imposed sanctions aimed at curtailing support for armed groups operating in the DRC. These sanctions target individuals and entities believed to be financing or supplying arms to rebels. While there have been calls for more robust interventions to stabilize the region, efforts have often been hampered by geopolitical interests and lack of consensus among international actors. Despite sanctions and international pressure, external support for rebel groups persists due to weak enforcement mechanisms and ongoing regional instability.

UAE And Darfurian Rebels

The financing of rebel groups by foreign governments is a critical issue in contemporary African conflicts, with significant implications for regional stability, governance, and resource management. Understanding this phenomenon is vital as it sheds light on the motivations behind foreign interventions and their consequences on local conflicts. The UAE's strategic interests in Africa, particularly regarding resource exploitation and geopolitical influence, underscore the complexity of these relationships.

The Darfur conflict began in February 2003 when two rebel groups, the Sudan Liberation Army/Movement (SLA/M) and the Justice and Equality Movement (JEM), launched a rebellion against the Sudanese government. The conflict arose from longstanding grievances related to economic marginalization and political disenfranchisement of non-Arab ethnic groups in Darfur. The Sudanese government's response involved enlisting Arab militias, leading to widespread violence and humanitarian crises that have claimed hundreds of thousands of lives and displaced millions.

The SLM/A was founded by members of indigenous ethnic groups in Darfur, primarily the Fur, Zaghawa, and Masalit. Initially established as the Darfur Liberation Front, it evolved into a significant player in the conflict, advocating for greater representation and rights for marginalized communities. The SLM/A has splintered into various factions over time, with differing strategies regarding peace negotiations and military engagement.

Sudan's geopolitical significance stems from its vast natural resources, including gold and agricultural land. The UAE's interest in these resources has intensified its involvement in Sudanese affairs. As Sudan navigates a complex political landscape marked by military coups and civil unrest, foreign powers like the UAE seek to leverage their influence to secure economic interests. The UAE's involvement in Libya has been characterized by support for Khalifa Haftar's Libyan National Army (LNA), which has implications for its interests in Darfur. Reports indicate that Darfurian rebel groups have received financial support from the UAE through their operations in Libya, where they engage in various military activities while profiting from local resources. This relationship highlights how conflicts can be interconnected across borders.

The UAE aims to expand its influence across Africa through strategic investments in agriculture, mining, and infrastructure. Its ambitions include securing access to key trade routes and resources vital for its economic diversification efforts. This strategy often involves backing local militias or rebel groups that can facilitate these objectives, as seen with its support for various factions within Sudan. The UAE's support for Darfurian rebels is driven by economic motivations linked to resource control. The region is rich in gold deposits; reports suggest that the SLM/A has exploited these resources to finance its operations. By supporting these groups, the UAE positions itself to benefit from lucrative mining opportunities while also gaining leverage over local politics. Access to gold mines is a primary motivation for foreign involvement in Sudanese conflicts. The UAE reportedly receives significant quantities of gold from Sudan, which is crucial for its economy. This extraction strategy underscores a broader trend where foreign powers engage with local conflicts primarily for resource acquisition rather than humanitarian concerns.

China And The Democratic Republic of Congo

The financing of rebel groups by foreign governments represents a significant challenge to stability and governance in Africa, particularly in resource rich nations like the Democratic Republic of the Congo (DRC). The DRC has faced chronic instability since gaining independence from Belgium in 1960. The country has been plagued by a series of conflicts, including two major wars (1996-1997 and 1998-2003) and ongoing violence involving numerous rebel groups, particularly in the eastern provinces. These conflicts are often fueled by ethnic tensions, competition for resources, and external interventions.

The evolution of foreign involvement in the DRC has been marked by fluctuating allegiances and interests. Historically, Western nations dominated the landscape, but China's increasing presence since the early 2000s has transformed this dynamic. The Chinese government has cultivated relationships with various political factions, leveraging its economic power to secure mining rights and infrastructure deals.

China's engagement with the DRC intensified under President Joseph Kabila, who sought alternative sources of investment following disappointing relations with Western donors. In 2008, China signed a landmark $9 billion deal with the DRC government, which provided funding for infrastructure development in exchange for access to mineral resources. This agreement marked a significant shift in China's approach, emphasizing non-interference in domestic politics and prioritizing economic gain over governance issues.

China's primary interest in the DRC lies in its vast mineral wealth, particularly cobalt, copper, and diamonds. The DRC produces approximately 80% of the world's cobalt supply, a critical component for batteries used in electronics and electric vehicles. As global demand for these technologies rises, so does China's reliance on Congolese resources. The strategic importance of these minerals is underscored by their role in global supply chains. Chinese state owned enterprises have established dominance over cobalt mining operations in the DRC, controlling significant portions of production and refining capacities. This control is essential for maintaining China's competitive edge in technology manufacturing.

China's support for rebel groups is often indirect but can manifest through various mechanisms. By investing heavily in mining operations controlled by local militias or rebel factions, China can indirectly finance these groups while securing resource extraction rights. Establishing relationships with local leaders who may have ties to rebel movements allows China to navigate complex political landscapes while promoting its economic interests. Reports indicate that China has provided military assistance to the Congolese government to combat rebel groups threatening Chinese investments. This involvement can further entrench existing conflicts. The implications of this financing extend beyond immediate economic benefits; they contribute to prolonged instability and undermine efforts toward peace and reconciliation within local communities.

Russia's Support For Armed Groups In The Central African Republic (CAR)

Foreign government involvement in African conflicts has increasingly become a focal point of international relations, particularly regarding the financing of rebel groups. This phenomenon raises critical questions about the implications for resource exploitation, local governance, and regional stability. The financing of armed groups often enables these factions to sustain prolonged conflicts that hinder development and exacerbate humanitarian crises.

The Central African Republic has endured decades of political instability characterized by coups, civil wars, and humanitarian crises. Since gaining independence from France in 1960, CAR has been plagued by a series of armed conflicts involving various rebel groups vying for control over the government and lucrative natural resources. The most recent civil war erupted in 2013, leading to widespread violence and displacement.

The Wagner Group emerged as a significant player in CAR's conflict landscape around 2018 when it began providing military support to President Faustin Archange Touadéra's government. This paramilitary organization is often described as a private military contractor, although its operations are closely aligned with Russian state interests. The group's activities include training local forces, providing security for government officials, and engaging in combat against rebel factions.

Historically, Russia has sought to re-establish its influence in Africa after decades of relative disengagement following the Soviet Union's collapse. The Kremlin views Africa as a strategic partner for securing natural resources essential for its economy, such as diamonds, gold, and uranium. This renewed interest is part of a broader strategy to counter Western influence on the continent and expand its geopolitical reach. Russia's support for rebel groups in CAR aligns with its geopolitical strategy of establishing friendly regimes that facilitate access to valuable resources. By backing armed factions like those associated with the Wagner Group, Russia can exert influence over local politics while ensuring that its economic interests are prioritized. Russia's actions in CAR reflect its broader foreign policy objectives aimed at countering Western hegemony and fostering alliances with governments that resist Western pressures. The Kremlin's engagement includes military assistance, diplomatic support, and economic investments that bolster regimes willing to cooperate with Russian interests.

International sanctions imposed on Russia due to its actions in Ukraine have further motivated the Kremlin to seek alternative revenue sources through resource extraction in Africa. By supporting rebel groups and securing mining rights in CAR, Russia can mitigate the economic impact of these sanctions while enhancing its global standing. The primary resources targeted by the Wagner Group and affiliated entities in CAR include diamonds, gold, and timber. These resources are not only vital for local economies but also serve as significant revenue sources for foreign actors involved in their extraction.

Wagner affiliated companies have been granted mining licenses and export authorizations that enable them to operate with relative impunity. For instance, companies like Lobaye Invest and Midas Ressources have established industrial scale gold production operations within CAR. These activities often occur without adequate oversight or benefit sharing with local communities. The exploitation of natural resources by foreign entities has profound implications for local economies. While it may generate short term revenue for certain factions or government officials, it often leads to long term environmental degradation and social unrest among communities that feel marginalized by these operations.

One notable case study involves Wagner's involvement in protecting diamond mines controlled by local warlords while providing military support to the CAR government. Reports indicate that Wagner mercenaries have engaged directly in combat against rival factions seeking control over these lucrative resources. Another example is Wagner's role in gold mining operations where they have reportedly facilitated illegal exports to finance their activities. These operations illustrate how foreign support can directly correlate with increased conflict intensity as groups vie for control over resource rich territories.

France In Mali And The Central African Republic

The historical ties between France and its former colonies in Africa are rooted in colonialism, which established a complex web of political, economic, and cultural relationships. After gaining independence in the mid-20th century, many African nations maintained close ties with France, often referred to as "Françafrique." This relationship has evolved, with France historically intervening in African conflicts to protect its interests and maintain influence.

Over the years, these ties have become increasingly strained due to rising anti-French sentiment fueled by perceptions of neocolonialism and ineffective governance. In recent years, countries like Mali and Burkina Faso have expelled French troops amid growing calls for sovereignty and self-determination. This backdrop sets the stage for understanding the motivations behind France's alleged support for rebel groups in these nations.

France's motivations for financing rebel groups in Mali and the Central African Republic (CAR) can be primarily linked to its economic interests, particularly in resource extraction. Both countries are rich in natural resources, including gold and diamonds, which are crucial for France's economic strategy. Reports indicate that French companies have engaged with armed groups to secure their operations amidst conflict. This financial support aligns with broader geopolitical strategies aimed at countering Russian influence in Africa, particularly through groups like the Wagner Group, which has been accused of exploiting local resources while destabilizing governments. By financing certain factions, France may aim to maintain a foothold in these resource rich regions while countering rival powers.

In Mali, various rebel groups have emerged amid ongoing conflict since 2012. The National Movement for the Liberation of Azawad (MNLA) and other factions have received varying degrees of support from foreign entities. Allegations suggest that France has provided indirect support to certain groups aligned with its interests, particularly those opposing jihadist factions.

In CAR, reports highlight that a subsidiary of the French Castel Group allegedly financed armed militias like the Union for Peace in the Central African Republic (UPC) to protect its sugar production interests. The group has been implicated in numerous human rights violations yet continues to operate due to this financial backing. The relationship illustrates how corporate interests can intertwine with military support.

El-Hadj Malick Sow

El-Hadj Malick Sow was a prominent Senegalese journalist known for his fearless reporting on political and social issues, particularly those involving police brutality and governmental corruption. He worked for several media outlets, including Walfadjri, where he gained recognition for his investigative journalism that often highlighted the struggles of ordinary Senegalese citizens against systemic injustices. Sow's commitment to uncovering the truth and advocating for press freedom made him a respected figure in the Senegalese media landscape.

Leading up to March 2020, Senegal experienced significant political tension characterized by widespread protests against police brutality and government corruption. The death of a young man, allegedly due to police violence, sparked nationwide demonstrations, reflecting growing public frustration with the government's handling of law enforcement and accountability. The political climate was charged, with many citizens demanding reforms to address issues of corruption and human rights abuses perpetrated by security forces.

On March 14th 2020, El-Hadj Malick Sow was covering protests in Dakar that erupted following the death of a young man at the hands of police. These protests were part of a larger movement against police violence and were marked by clashes between demonstrators and law enforcement. Eyewitness accounts describe Sow as actively reporting from the front lines of the protests when he was struck by a police vehicle. Reports indicate that he was severely injured and subsequently died from his injuries. While official statements from law enforcement characterized the incident as an accident, many witnesses disputed this narrative, suggesting that there was intent involved.

The immediate public reaction to Sow's death was one of outrage and grief. Protests erupted across Senegal, with demonstrators demanding justice for Sow and accountability for police actions. His death resonated deeply within the community, serving as a catalyst for renewed calls for reform regarding police conduct and press freedom. Sow's murder highlighted the precarious position of journalists in Senegal, particularly those who challenge authority or report on sensitive topics such as police violence. The incident intensified discussions about press freedom in the country, with many advocating for stronger protections for journalists who face threats while performing their duties.

In response to Sow's death, government officials expressed condolences; however, many activists criticized the lack of concrete action regarding accountability for police violence. Law enforcement agencies conducted an internal investigation into the incident, but skepticism remained regarding its impartiality and effectiveness.Subsequent legal actions were limited, with few tangible outcomes reported in terms of accountability for those responsible for Sow's death. The lack of transparency in investigations into violence against journalists further fueled public distrust in governmental institutions.

Adame Pardo

Salvador Adame Pardo was a Mexican journalist whose work primarily focused on issues related to drug cartels and local corruption. Operating in a perilous environment, Adame Pardo served as the director of Canal 6, a television station in Michoacan, where he reported on the rampant violence and criminal activities associated with organized crime. His contributions to journalism were significant, as they shed light on the dangers faced by communities under the influence of drug trafficking organizations. Tragically, Adame Pardo was kidnapped and murdered on June 14th 2017, a stark reminder of the threats that journalists encounter in Mexico.

Salvador Adame Pardo had a notable career in journalism, particularly recognized for his fearless reporting at Canal 6. He covered various topics, including local politics and crime, but his focus on organized crime made him particularly vulnerable. His investigative work often exposed corruption and violence linked to drug cartels operating in Michoacan, a state notorious for its high levels of criminal activity. The broader landscape of journalism in Mexico is fraught with danger. Over the past decade, Mexico has consistently ranked as one of the most dangerous countries for journalists. According to the Committee to Protect Journalists (CPJ), at least 47 journalists were killed between 2010 and 2020 due to their work. The risks associated with reporting on organized crime are exacerbated by a culture of impunity; many perpetrators of violence against journalists face no legal consequences.

On May 18th 2017, Salvador Adame Pardo was kidnapped by armed men in Nueva Italia, Michoacan. His abduction occurred shortly after he had reported on local drug trafficking activities. Following his disappearance, there was widespread concern for his safety among colleagues and human rights organizations. On June 14th 2017, his charred remains were discovered along a roadside in Michoacan. The Attorney General's office confirmed that his body had been burned by members of organized crime. This brutal act highlighted the extreme risks faced by journalists who dare to expose the truth about criminal enterprises.

Adame Pardo's murder sent shockwaves through the journalism community in Mexico. It underscored the lethal consequences that can arise from reporting on sensitive topics such as drug trafficking and corruption. His death not only represented a personal tragedy but also reflected the systemic issues that place journalists at risk. The immediate reactions to Adame Pardo's murder were marked by outrage from media organizations, human rights groups, and the public. Protests erupted demanding justice for him and accountability for those responsible for violence against journalists. His killing became emblematic of the ongoing dangers faced by reporters covering organized crime.

President Barack Obama And Assata Shakur

Assata Shakur, born JoAnne Deborah Byron in 1947, is a significant figure in American history, known for her role as a political activist and member of the Black Liberation Army (BLA). She gained notoriety after being convicted of the murder of New Jersey State Trooper Werner Foerster during a 1973 traffic stop that resulted in a violent confrontation. Shakur's trial was marked by controversy, with many arguing that she did not receive a fair trial due to systemic racism and political bias. In 1979, she escaped from prison and sought asylum in Cuba, where she has lived ever since.

In 2013, the FBI placed Shakur on its Most Wanted Terrorists list and increased the bounty for her capture to $2 million, marking a significant moment in her ongoing status as a fugitive. Assata Shakur's flight from justice began after the aforementioned incident in 1973, which led to her arrest and subsequent conviction for murder in 1977. The socio-political climate during her trial was charged with racial tensions and civil rights struggles, as the Black Panther Party and similar organizations faced intense scrutiny and repression from law enforcement. The FBI's COINTELPRO program aimed to undermine these groups, labeling activists like Shakur as terrorists. Following her escape in 1979, Shakur found refuge in Cuba, where she has remained a symbol of resistance against systemic oppression. Her actions and subsequent asylum highlight the complexities surrounding race, justice, and political dissent in America.

During his presidency, Barack Obama implemented various criminal justice reforms aimed at addressing systemic inequalities within the justice system. However, his administration also faced criticism for its handling of political activists. The decision to raise the bounty on Shakur can be viewed through this lens; it reflects a continuation of efforts to apprehend individuals labeled as terrorists or threats to national security. The motivations behind this decision may include appeasing law enforcement agencies seeking closure for high profile cases and responding to ongoing public interest in Shakur's legacy as a polarizing figure.

The announcement regarding the increased bounty was made on May 2nd 2013, coinciding with the 40th anniversary of the shootout that led to Foerster's death. This timing was significant, as it reignited public discourse around Shakur's actions and their implications for civil rights movements. Key figures involved included FBI officials who emphasized the need to bring Shakur to justice. Public reaction was mixed; while some supported the government's actions as necessary for accountability, others viewed it as an attack on political dissent and an attempt to silence revolutionary voices. The raised bounty had several immediate impacts on Shakur's life and her supporters. For Shakur, it reaffirmed her status as a fugitive and intensified scrutiny on her activities in

Cuba. For her supporters, it galvanized efforts to defend her legacy and challenge narratives that paint her solely as a criminal. Additionally, this move had broader implications for U.S.-Cuba relations. By designating Shakur as a terrorist harboring in Cuba, the U.S. government sought to justify its ongoing embargo against the island nation and reinforce its stance against perceived threats from leftist movements.

Michael Hastings

Whistleblowing is the act of exposing information or activities deemed illegal, unethical, or not in the public interest, often involving individuals within organizations who reveal misconduct to authorities or the public. This practice is significant for promoting transparency and accountability, particularly in government and corporate sectors. It serves as a crucial mechanism for safeguarding democratic values and ensuring that those in power are held accountable for their actions.

Michael Hastings, an American investigative journalist, epitomized the role of a whistleblower through his fearless reporting on military and political corruption. Known for his incisive critiques and unyielding dedication to uncovering the truth, Hastings' work not only influenced public discourse but also highlighted the risks faced by journalists who dare to challenge authority.

Michael Mahon Hastings was born on January 28th 1980, in Malone, New York. He grew up in Burlington, Vermont, where he attended Rice Memorial High School before pursuing higher education at New York University, graduating in 2002. Hastings began his career at Newsweek, where he gained recognition for his coverage of the Iraq War. His personal experiences deeply informed his journalism; notably, his fiancee, Andrea Parhamovich, was killed in a car bombing in Baghdad in 2007, an event that profoundly impacted his life and work.

Hastings authored several notable works that examined military and political corruption. His book; I Lost My Love in Baghdad: A Modern War Story, recounts his experiences surrounding Parhamovich's death and critiques the realities of war. He is perhaps best known for his explosive 2010 article "The Runaway General," published in Rolling Stone, which revealed damaging comments made by General Stanley McChrystal and ultimately led to the general's resignation.

Hastings' investigative journalism focused significantly on the wars in Afghanistan and Iraq. His reporting was characterized by a commitment to uncovering uncomfortable truths about military operations and leadership. In "The Runaway General," Hastings provided an unprecedented look into McChrystal's command style and the culture within the U.S. military leadership, illustrating how informal conversations among officers could undermine official narratives. Hastings also wrote extensively about issues such as drone warfare and military policy, challenging the prevailing narratives that often sanitized the realities of conflict. His work had a profound impact on public perception regarding military operations and contributed to debates about U.S. foreign policy. By exposing corruption and incompetence within military ranks, Hastings played a crucial role in shaping discussions around accountability and oversight.

On June 18th 2013, Michael Hastings died tragically in a single vehicle car crash in Los Angeles at approximately 4:30 AM. Witnesses reported that his car was traveling at high speed before it struck a tree and burst into flames. The official investigation concluded that Hastings' death was accidental; however, many expressed skepticism about the circumstances surrounding the crash due to his controversial reporting and high profile connections.

In the aftermath of his death, questions arose regarding whether Hastings' investigative work had made him a target. Some speculated that he may have been under surveillance or faced threats from powerful entities unhappy with his revelations. Various theories emerged following Hastings' death, including claims of foul play orchestrated by government or military officials seeking retribution for his reporting. These theories were fueled by Hastings' own statements about feeling threatened prior to his death. In interviews, he had expressed concerns over potential repercussions from powerful figures he had exposed through his journalism.

Andrew Breitbart

Andrew Breitbart was a prominent American conservative commentator and journalist known for his provocative style and influential role in political discourse. Born on February 1st 1969, in Los Angeles, California, Breitbart became a key figure in conservative media, founding Breitbart News and playing a pivotal role in various high profile controversies. His work not only shaped public opinion but also highlighted the risks faced by those who challenge powerful institutions. Andrew Breitbart's investigative work was marked by his aggressive tactics and willingness to confront established organizations. He gained national attention for his role in exposing corruption within organizations such as ACORN (Association of Community Organizations for Reform Now) and Planned Parenthood. In 2009, Breitbart released a series of undercover videos featuring ACORN employees providing advice to individuals posing as a pimp and a prostitute. This expose led to widespread condemnation of ACORN, resulting in Congress voting to defund the organization.

Breitbart utilized undercover videos as a primary method for his investigations, believing that visual evidence could effectively sway public opinion. His approach was controversial; while many conservatives praised him for exposing wasteful government spending and unethical practices, critics accused him of engaging in entrapment and misrepresentation. His work on the Anthony Weiner sexting scandal further solidified his reputation as a formidable adversary of liberal politics, culminating in Weiner's resignation from Congress.

Andrew Breitbart's sudden death on March 1st 2012, at the age of 43 shocked many. He died from heart failure shortly after attending a party in Los Angeles. The official cause of death was attributed to natural causes; however, speculation surrounding his demise quickly emerged due to his controversial work and the enemies he made throughout his career. In the days following his death, conspiracy theories circulated suggesting foul play might have been involved. Some supporters claimed that his outspoken criticism of powerful figures could have put him at risk.

Gary Webb

Gary Webb, an American investigative journalist, is best known for his groundbreaking work that exposed alleged connections between the CIA and drug trafficking in the United States. His series "Dark Alliance," published in 1996, linked the crack cocaine epidemic in Los Angeles to CIA supported Contra rebels in Nicaragua. Webb's contributions to investigative journalism highlighted systemic issues within government operations and raised critical questions about accountability.

Gary Stephen Webb was born on August 31st 1955, in Corona, California. He began his journalism career at small newspapers in Kentucky and Ohio before joining the San Jose Mercury News in 1988. Webb's early work included coverage of the Loma Prieta earthquake, which contributed to the newspaper's Pulitzer Prize winning reporting. Webb's most significant contribution came with the publication of the "Dark Alliance" series in August 1996. This three part investigation claimed that CIA backed Contra rebels were involved in drug trafficking operations that contributed to the crack cocaine epidemic devastating African American communities in Los Angeles. The series detailed how profits from cocaine sales were allegedly funneled to support Contra activities against the Sandinista government in Nicaragua. Webb's findings sparked outrage and led to multiple investigations into the allegations. The implications of Webb's work were profound, as it suggested complicity by U.S. government agencies in drug trafficking activities that had catastrophic effects on urban communities. Despite initial acclaim for his reporting, Webb faced significant backlash from mainstream media outlets that questioned his conclusions and methodologies.

Whistleblowers like Gary Webb face numerous risks when exposing corruption or misconduct. These risks include threats to their safety, damage to their reputations, and severe professional consequences. The backlash against whistleblowers can manifest as public vilification, loss of employment, or even legal repercussions. Other notable whistleblowers have faced similar fates for their revelations. Edward Snowden, for instance, leaked classified information about NSA surveillance practices and has since lived in exile due to fears of prosecution. Chelsea Manning disclosed sensitive military documents related to U.S. operations in Iraq and Afghanistan, resulting in imprisonment and ongoing struggles with mental health after her release. These cases illustrate the high stakes involved in whistleblowing and raise questions about the protections available for individuals who expose wrongdoing.

On December 10th 2004, Gary Webb was found dead at his home in Sacramento, California. His death was ruled a suicide by gunshot; however, circumstances surrounding his demise have led to widespread speculation and controversy. Many supporters believe that Webb's death was not merely a suicide but rather a consequence of his investigative work and the powerful enemies he made throughout his career. Public reaction to Webb's death included conspiracy theories suggesting foul play due to his controversial reporting on government corruption and drug trafficking.

The long term effects of Gary Webb's investigative work are evident in public discourse surrounding government accountability and drug policies. His "Dark Alliance" series prompted national conversations about the impact of U.S. foreign policy on domestic issues such as drug addiction and crime.

In response to public outcry following Webb's revelations, several investigations were initiated into the CIA's activities during the Contra war. While some findings corroborated aspects of Webb's reporting, such as links between Contra funding and drug trafficking, mainstream media largely dismissed his conclusions as exaggerated or conspiratorial.

Barack Obama

The Blue Alert Law, formally known as the Rafael Ramos and Wenjian Liu National Blue Alert Act of 2015, was signed into law by President Barack Obama on May 19th 2015. This legislation aims to establish a nationwide system for alerting the public and law enforcement about threats to police officers, particularly in cases where officers are killed, seriously injured, or missing in connection with their duties. The law is significant in the context of rising concerns over police safety and public perceptions of police brutality in the United States. The significance of police brutality has been a critical issue in American society, especially in light of high profile incidents that have sparked national protests and discussions about systemic racism and law enforcement practices. The Blue Alert Law was enacted during a period marked by heightened tensions between police forces and communities, particularly following events in Ferguson, Missouri, and other cities that highlighted issues of racial injustice.

The introduction of the Blue Alert Law was influenced by several key events leading up to its passage. The immediate catalyst was the ambush killing of NYPD officers Rafael Ramos and Wenjian Liu on December 20th 2014. Prior to the Blue Alert Law, various pieces of legislation aimed at regulating police conduct and protecting citizen rights existed. For instance, the Violent Crime Control and Law Enforcement Act of 1994 included provisions for community policing but did not directly address officer safety in the context of public alerts.

The law aims to prevent police brutality indirectly by fostering an environment where law enforcement personnel feel safer and more supported. By quickly disseminating information about threats to officers, it seeks to enhance public cooperation in apprehending suspects who pose risks to police safety. While the Blue Alert Law primarily focuses on protecting law enforcement personnel, its implications for victims of police brutality are complex. Critics argue that such laws may inadvertently reinforce a culture that prioritizes officer safety over accountability for police misconduct. For individuals who experience violence at the hands of law enforcement, the heightened focus on alerts for officer safety may limit their ability to seek justice and defend their rights. Additionally, there are concerns that laws emphasizing protection for officers could lead to increased militarization of police responses during protests or civil unrest, potentially exacerbating tensions between communities and law enforcement.

Edgar Daniel Esquivel

Edgar Daniel Esquivel was a dedicated journalist known for his courageous reporting on police corruption and violence in Mexico. His work focused on exposing the links between law enforcement and organized crime, which put him at great personal risk. Esquivel's commitment to uncovering the truth exemplified the challenges faced by journalists in a country where freedom of the press is severely compromised.

On February 22nd 2018, Edgar Daniel Esquivel was shot while covering an event in Veracruz, Mexico. The incident occurred during a public gathering that was ostensibly peaceful but was marred by underlying tensions related to local governance and crime. Esquivel was known to have received threats prior to his death due to his investigative work, particularly concerning police corruption in the region. His shooting highlighted the extreme dangers faced by journalists who dare to report on issues that challenge powerful interests. The event he was covering at the time of the incident was significant; it involved local politicians and community leaders discussing public safety, an ironic backdrop given Esquivel's own fate. His presence at this gathering underscored his commitment to reporting on issues that were critical to the community's welfare.

Esquivel's work had a profound influence on discussions surrounding media integrity in Mexico. By exposing police corruption and violence, he contributed significantly to raising awareness about the systemic issues plaguing Mexican society. His reporting not only informed the public but also served as a catalyst for dialogue about accountability within law enforcement agencies.

The public and governmental responses to Esquivel's shooting were mixed. While there were calls for justice from civil society organizations and fellow journalists demanding accountability, government action was often perceived as insufficient. The lack of thorough investigations into his murder reflected a troubling trend in Mexico, where many crimes against media workers remain unresolved.

Javier Valdez Cardenas

Javier Valdez Cardenas was a prominent Mexican journalist whose work focused on drug trafficking and organized crime, particularly in the context of Sinaloa, a region notorious for its drug cartels. Born on April 14th 1967, in Culiacan, Sinaloa, Valdez graduated with a degree in sociology from the Autonomous University of Sinaloa. His career began in the early 1990s as a reporter for local television and newspapers, eventually leading to the co-founding of Riodoce in 2003, an independent weekly that became known for its fearless reporting on crime and corruption in one of Mexico's most violent states. Valdez authored several influential books, including Miss Narco and Los morros del narco, which explored the impact of drug trafficking on society. His commitment to investigative journalism earned him numerous accolades, including the International Press Freedom Award from the Committee to Protect Journalists in 2011.

The socio-political environment of Sinaloa during Valdez's career was marked by extreme violence and corruption linked to powerful drug cartels, particularly the Sinaloa Cartel led by Joaquin "El Chapo" Guzman. Journalists operating in this landscape faced significant challenges, including threats to their safety, censorship, and the pervasive influence of organized crime on local governance. The climate of fear often resulted in self-censorship among media professionals, as many were hesitant to cover sensitive topics due to potential reprisals from criminal groups. Valdez's work was a stark contrast to this trend; he consistently reported on the realities of drug trafficking and its effects on communities. His investigations into police corruption and cartel activities made him a target for those who sought to silence dissenting voices. The dangers he faced were emblematic of the broader risks confronting journalists in Mexico, where violence against media workers has reached alarming levels.

On May 15th 2017, Javier Valdez Cardenas was brutally murdered outside a post office near the offices of Riodoce in Culiacan. He was shot twelve times by unidentified gunmen who ambushed him shortly after he left his workplace. The attackers dragged him from his vehicle and fled in his car after stealing his laptop and mobile phone. This heinous act occurred in broad daylight, underscoring the audacity of organized crime in targeting journalists. Prior to his murder, Valdez had received multiple death threats related to his reporting on drug cartels and corruption. Despite these threats, he remained committed to his work, famously stating that he would not cease writing even if it meant risking his life. His assassination shocked not only the local community but also drew international condemnation from human rights organizations and press freedom advocates.

Miroslava Breach Velducea

Miroslava Breach Velducea was a prominent Mexican journalist known for her fearless reporting on corruption, drug trafficking, and human rights violations in the northern state of Chihuahua. Born on August 7th 1962, in Chinipas, Chihuahua, she pursued a degree in Political Science and Public Administration before embarking on a two decade long career in journalism. Breach worked as a correspondent for the national newspaper La Jornada and contributed to several local outlets, including Norte de Juarez. Her investigative work was significant in exposing the intricate connections between organized crime and local politics, making her a target in a country where violence against journalists is rampant. Breach's commitment to uncovering the truth underscored the vital role of journalism in promoting accountability and transparency in Mexico.

Miroslava Breach's investigative journalism focused primarily on exposing corruption within local governments and the pervasive influence of drug cartels. One of her most notable reports was published in March 2016, where she revealed that cartel members had infiltrated mayoral candidate lists for major political parties in Chihuahua. This investigation highlighted the dangerous intersection of politics and organized crime, particularly in rural areas plagued by drug related violence.

Breach's reporting not only informed the public but also prompted governmental responses. For instance, her revelations about former Governor Cesar Duarte's corruption, where she detailed embezzlement of 900 million pesos, led to national outrage and calls for accountability. Her work raised awareness about critical issues such as forced disappearances, environmental degradation caused by illegal logging, and the plight of indigenous communities affected by organized crime. The impact of her journalism was profound, as it brought critical issues to light and challenged authorities to act against corruption and violence.

Throughout her career, Miroslava Breach faced numerous threats due to her reporting on sensitive topics. Despite these dangers, she continued her work with unwavering resolve. The broader context of violence against journalists in Mexico is alarming; according to various reports, Mexico is one of the deadliest countries for journalists, with over 90% of crimes against them remaining unpunished. In 2017 alone, six journalists were murdered in Mexico, illustrating the severe risks faced by those who dare to speak out against powerful interests. Breach received direct threats related to her investigations into drug trafficking and political corruption. These threats were indicative of a climate of fear that silenced many journalists across the country. The lack of effective protection mechanisms for journalists further exacerbated this issue, leaving many vulnerable to violence.

On March 23rd 2017, Miroslava Breach was assassinated outside her home in Chihuahua City while dropping off her son at school. She was shot multiple times by assailants who approached her vehicle. The brutal nature of her murder shocked the nation and drew widespread condemnation from media organizations and human rights advocates. Following her death, there were immediate calls for justice from both the public and government officials, emphasizing the need to address the increasing violence against journalists. The media reaction was swift; many outlets mourned her loss while highlighting the dangers faced by reporters in Mexico. Editorials called for stronger protections for journalists and accountability for those who perpetrate violence against them.

In the aftermath of Miroslava Breach's murder, investigations were launched by various authorities, including the federal Special Prosecutor for Attention to Crimes against Freedom of Expression (FEADLE). Initial investigations identified suspects linked to organized crime groups that had motives related to Breach's reporting. Significant progress was made when Juan Carlos Moreno Ochoa, alias El Larry, was arrested and convicted for his role in orchestrating Breach's murder. He received a sentence of 50 years in prison in August 2020. Additionally, Hugo Amed Schultz Alcaraz, a former mayor implicated in facilitating information about Breach to criminal organizations, was sentenced to eight years in prison following a plea deal.

Donald Trump

The Central Park Five case refers to the wrongful conviction of five Black and Latino teenagers; Kevin Richardson, Antron McCray, Raymond Santana, Korey Wise, and Yusef Salaam, who were accused of raping a white woman, Trisha Meili, in Central Park in April 1989. Following intense media scrutiny and public outrage, these teenagers were coerced into giving false confessions and ultimately convicted. The case highlighted significant flaws in the criminal justice system, particularly regarding race, police conduct, and media influence.

In the wake of this incident, Donald Trump, then a prominent real estate developer in New York City, took out full page advertisements in four major newspapers calling for the reinstatement of the death penalty. This advertisement was published shortly after the attack and is widely perceived as a reaction to the heightened fear surrounding crime in New York City at that time.

Trump's advertisement was published on May 1st 1989, in the New York Times, New York Daily News, New York Post, and Newsday. The ad featured bold headlines that read "Bring Back the Death Penalty. Bring Back Our Police!" Trump argued for harsher penalties for violent criminals and expressed his belief that those responsible for heinous acts should face severe consequences. The content of the ad did not mention the Central Park Five by name; however, it was clear that it was aimed at the suspects in this high profile case. The ad tapped into public fears about crime and positioned Trump as a strong advocate for law enforcement. The immediate media reaction included both support from those who shared his views on crime and criticism from civil rights advocates who saw it as inflammatory and prejudicial.

Trump's motivations for placing the ad can be understood within the context of his public persona at that time. In 1989, he was not yet a national political figure but was known for his brash style and willingness to engage in controversial issues. The Central Park Jogger case had captured national attention, and Trump sought to align himself with public sentiment that demanded justice for Meili while also appealing to fears about rising crime rates in New York City. His decision can be seen as an attempt to position himself as a tough on crime advocate, which would later become a hallmark of his political career. By taking such a strong stance publicly, he aimed to enhance his profile within New York's political landscape.

The advertisement had profound implications for public perception of the Central Park Five. By calling for extreme measures against violent offenders, Trump contributed to an environment that presumed guilt before trial. This narrative likely influenced jurors and public opinion against the five teenagers, exacerbating racial tensions and undermining their right to a fair trial. The legal repercussions were significant; although Trump's ad did not directly lead to their convictions, it played a role in shaping an atmosphere where racial profiling and wrongful accusations could thrive. The five were convicted based largely on coerced confessions obtained under duress during lengthy interrogations without legal representation.

Regina Martinez Perez

Regina Martinez Perez was a dedicated journalist whose work highlighted critical social issues and corruption in Mexico. Born on July 13th 1964, in the small town of Xalapa, Veracruz, she pursued a career in journalism that spanned over three decades. Martinez became a correspondent for the national magazine Proceso, where she gained recognition for her fearless reporting on drug related violence and political corruption. Her work was particularly significant in the context of Veracruz, a state deeply affected by organized crime and government complicity. Martinez's commitment to uncovering the truth made her a vital voice in Mexican journalism, one that ultimately cost her life.

Martinez's journalistic career began in local newspapers before she joined Proceso in 2000. Throughout her career, she focused on various pressing issues, including human rights abuses, environmental concerns, and the pervasive influence of drug cartels on local politics. Notable among her articles were investigations into the links between organized crime and government officials, particularly during a time when Veracruz was experiencing escalating violence due to drug trafficking. One of her significant reports involved the arrest of nine police officers accused of colluding with drug cartels. Additionally, she covered the arrest of Comandante Chaparro, a high ranking member of the Zetas cartel. These articles not only informed the public but also challenged local authorities, exposing their connections to criminal organizations. Her critical stance against government corruption made her an essential figure in advocating for accountability and transparency. Martinez was known for her investigative rigor and her ability to navigate dangerous environments to report on stories that others avoided. Colleagues described her as someone who went beyond traditional reporting; she immersed herself in the communities she covered, giving voice to marginalized groups and shedding light on issues often overlooked by mainstream media.

On April 28th 2012, Regina Martinez was found murdered in her home in Xalapa. She had been brutally beaten and strangled, with signs indicating a violent struggle. Her death occurred just days after she published several articles that highlighted corruption and violence in Veracruz, raising suspicions that her murder was linked to her journalistic work. The impact of Martinez's death reverberated throughout the journalistic community and society at large. It underscored the dangers faced by journalists in Mexico, particularly those covering organized crime and corruption. Colleagues expressed their shock and fear, recognizing that her murder was not an isolated incident but part of a broader pattern of violence against journalists in the country.

Yessenia Mollinedo

Yessenia Mollinedo was a dedicated journalist whose work focused on the pressing social issues and rampant corruption in Mexico, particularly within law enforcement. Born in Veracruz, she became the director of El Veraz, a local news outlet that aimed to provide transparent journalism in a region plagued by violence and crime. Her commitment to uncovering the truth made her a significant figure in Mexican journalism, especially as the country faced increasing threats against press freedom. Tragically, Mollinedo's life was cut short when she was murdered on May 9th 2022, highlighting the severe risks journalists face in Mexico.

Yessenia Mollinedo began her career in journalism with a focus on crime reporting and social issues that affected her community. As the founder and editor of El Veraz, she utilized the platform to investigate local corruption, particularly within law enforcement agencies. Her reporting often addressed the pervasive influence of drug cartels and the complicity of police officials, which resonated deeply with local communities seeking accountability. Mollinedo's articles frequently exposed the failures of local authorities to protect citizens from violence and crime. For instance, she reported on cases involving police misconduct and the connections between law enforcement and organized crime. Her fearless approach to journalism earned her respect among peers but also drew significant attention from those who preferred to keep such issues hidden. Despite facing numerous threats over her career, Mollinedo remained committed to her work until her untimely death. She had previously reported receiving death threats, prompting her to modify her reporting style and limit coverage on particularly dangerous topics.

Mollinedo's reporting had a profound impact on local communities in Veracruz. By shedding light on corruption within law enforcement, she empowered citizens to demand accountability from their leaders. Her work not only informed the public about ongoing issues but also fostered a sense of community activism against corruption and violence. The broader implications of Mollinedo's work extend to journalism in regions affected by drug related violence. In Mexico, where more than 150 journalists have been murdered since 2000, her case reflects the dangerous environment for reporters. The Committee to Protect Journalists (CPJ) noted that Mexico is one of the deadliest countries for journalists in the Western Hemisphere, with at least 36 murders during President Andres Manuel Lopez Obrador's administration alone. Mollinedo's reporting exemplified the critical role journalists play in exposing injustices, even as they face life threatening risks.

On May 9th 2022, Yessenia Mollinedo was shot dead alongside fellow journalist Sheila Johana Garcia while they were sitting in a car outside a convenience store in Cosoleacaque, Veracruz. This brutal act occurred just days after Mollinedo had reported receiving death threats while covering events related to Children's Day. Eyewitness accounts indicated that unidentified assailants approached their vehicle and opened fire without hesitation. Mollinedo's murder occurred against a backdrop of escalating violence against journalists in Mexico. Just days before her death, another journalist, Luis Enrique Ramirez, was also killed, underscoring a troubling pattern of targeted attacks against those who dare to report on sensitive issues such as crime and corruption.

Mordechai Vanunu

Mordechai Vanunu, an Israeli nuclear technician, is one of the most prominent whistleblowers in history. His revelations about Israel's nuclear weapons program in 1986 not only exposed critical information about nuclear proliferation but also demonstrated the extreme consequences that whistleblowers can face.

The Cold War era was marked by intense competition between superpowers, particularly the United States and the Soviet Union, leading to a global arms race that included the development of nuclear weapons. During this period, many nations pursued nuclear capabilities, often shrouded in secrecy. Israel's nuclear program, centered at the Dimona facility, was particularly opaque, with the government denying the existence of nuclear weapons despite widespread suspicions.

Mordechai Vanunu worked as a technician at the Dimona facility from 1976 until 1985. In November 1985, he was laid off during a mass reduction of staff but remained concerned about Israel's nuclear ambitions. In September 1986, he provided detailed information to The Sunday Times, revealing that Israel possessed at least 200 nuclear warheads and had developed sophisticated nuclear capabilities. His disclosures were significant as they contradicted Israel's long standing policy of ambiguity regarding its nuclear arsenal. Vanunu's revelations raised critical questions about global nuclear policy and nonproliferation efforts. They prompted discussions on the need for greater transparency among nations possessing nuclear weapons and highlighted the potential dangers posed by unregulated nuclear proliferation.

Mordechai Vanunu's decision to leak information about Israel's nuclear program stemmed from his moral opposition to weapons of mass destruction. He believed that the international community had a right to know about Israel's capabilities and that transparency was essential for global security. To document his claims, Vanunu secretly took 57 photographs inside the Dimona facility using a smuggled camera. After leaving Israel for Australia in 1986, he contacted The Sunday Times journalist Peter Hounam to share his findings. The resulting article published on October 5th 1986, titled "Revealed: The Secrets of Israel's Nuclear Arsenal," detailed the extent of Israel's nuclear capabilities and sparked international debate about its implications for regional security. Vanunu's disclosures had profound implications for global nuclear policy. They challenged the notion of state secrecy surrounding national security issues and underscored the importance of whistleblowing in holding governments accountable for their actions regarding weapons of mass destruction.

Shortly after his revelations were published, Vanunu was kidnapped by agents from Mossad while in Italy. Lured under false pretenses to Rome, he was drugged and forcibly returned to Israel aboard a naval vessel.

Upon his return, he faced charges of treason and espionage in a trial held behind closed doors. In March 1988, he was convicted and sentenced to 18 years in prison, with more than eleven years spent in solitary confinement. The legal repercussions did not end with his imprisonment; even after serving his sentence and being released in 2004, Vanunu faced ongoing restrictions on his freedom. Israeli authorities imposed military orders that limited his ability to travel abroad, communicate with foreigners, or speak freely to journalists. These punitive measures were justified by officials as necessary for national security but have been widely criticized as retribution for his whistleblowing actions.

Amnesty International has labeled Vanunu a prisoner of conscience, arguing that he has been subjected to vindictive treatment for exercising his right to free expression. His case exemplifies the severe consequences that whistleblowers can face when challenging powerful state interests.

Bradley Manning

Bradley Edward Manning was born on December 17th 1987, and is one of the most notable whistleblowers in recent history. As a U.S. Army intelligence analyst, Manning leaked classified documents to WikiLeaks in 2010, revealing critical information about U.S. military operations in Iraq and Afghanistan. His actions sparked a global debate about government transparency, national security and the ethical implications of whistleblowing.

Bradley Manning was born in Crescent, Oklahoma, and raised in a military family. After high school, he joined the U.S. Army in 2007 and was trained as an intelligence analyst. Manning was deployed to Iraq in 2009, where he had access to classified military databases. During his time in Iraq, Manning became increasingly disillusioned with the military's operations and the treatment of civilians during conflicts. He witnessed firsthand the consequences of war and began to collect evidence of what he believed were serious human rights violations committed by U.S. forces.

The classified documents Manning leaked included nearly 750,000 military and diplomatic files, which came to be known as the "Iraq War Logs," "Afghan War Diary," and "Guantanamo files." Among these documents was a video titled "Collateral Murder," which depicted a U.S. helicopter attack that killed a group of people in Baghdad, including two Reuters journalists. The footage raised significant ethical questions regarding the rules of engagement used by U.S. forces. Manning's leaks also revealed instances of torture and abuse by U.S. personnel at facilities like Abu Ghraib and highlighted the broader implications of U.S. foreign policy in Iraq and Afghanistan. The revelations prompted widespread media coverage and public outrage, leading to discussions about the need for greater accountability within the military.

In early 2010, Manning began communicating with WikiLeaks founder Julian Assange through encrypted online chats. He shared his concerns about U.S. military operations and expressed his desire to expose what he viewed as wrongdoing. After gathering substantial evidence over several months, he decided to leak the documents to WikiLeaks. Manning's decision to leak classified information was driven by his moral conviction that the public had a right to know about potential human rights abuses committed by their government. He believed that transparency could foster informed debate on U.S. military actions.

The immediate reaction from the U.S. government was one of alarm and condemnation. Military officials characterized Manning's actions as a grave breach of national security that endangered lives and compromised ongoing operations. In May 2010, Manning was arrested in Iraq after former hacker Adrian Lamo reported him to authorities. Manning faced charges under the Espionage Act and other offenses related to unauthorized disclosure of classified information. His trial began in June 2013 amid intense media scrutiny and public interest.

The global response to Manning's leaks was mixed. While some hailed him as a hero for exposing government wrongdoing, others viewed him as a traitor who jeopardized national security. Major news outlets like The New York Times, The Guardian, and Der Spiegel published extensive coverage of the leaked documents, contributing to public discourse on government accountability. Public opinion varied widely; many activists supported Manning's actions as essential for democracy, while others criticized her for compromising sensitive information that could endanger lives.

Bradley Manning faced severe legal consequences for her actions. In July 2013, she was convicted on 17 counts related to leaking classified information but acquitted of aiding the enemy, a charge that could have resulted in a life sentence or death penalty. Ultimately, she was sentenced to 35 years in prison, one of the longest sentences ever imposed for leaking information to the media. Manning's treatment during incarceration drew widespread criticism from human rights organizations such as Amnesty International and Human Rights Watch, which described it as cruel and degrading. He spent nearly two years at Quantico Marine Corps Brig under harsh conditions before being transferred to a civilian prison.

Anna Politkovskaya

Anna Politkovskaya, a prominent Russian journalist, exemplified the courage and commitment required to expose the truth in the face of severe danger. Born on August 30th 1958, in New York City to Soviet-Ukrainian parents, she became renowned for her investigative reporting on human rights abuses during the Second Chechen War. Her unwavering dedication to uncovering the harsh realities of war and oppression made her a target for those in power.

The Chechen conflict has deep historical roots dating back to the 18th century but gained prominence following the dissolution of the Soviet Union in 1991. After declaring independence from Russia in 1991, Chechnya experienced two brutal wars with Russian forces, first from 1994 to 1996 and then from 1999 to 2009. The Second Chechen War began under President Vladimir Putin's administration and was characterized by widespread human rights violations committed by both Russian troops and Chechen separatists. During this period, civilians suffered immensely due to military operations, forced disappearances, torture, and extrajudicial killings. Reports indicated that Russian forces employed tactics such as mass bombings and indiscriminate violence against civilian populations. The conflict also led to significant displacement, with thousands fleeing their homes to escape the violence.

Anna Politkovskaya emerged as a prominent voice documenting the atrocities occurring during the

Second Chechen War. Writing for Novaya Gazeta, she published numerous articles detailing human rights abuses committed by Russian soldiers and highlighting the plight of civilians caught in the crossfire. Her investigative work included firsthand accounts from survivors of violence, interviews with families of victims, and exposure of war crimes that often went unreported by mainstream media. One notable report described the horrors faced by civilians during a Russian military operation in Grozny. Politkovskaya's writing was characterized by its emotional depth and commitment to truth telling; she sought to humanize victims often reduced to mere statistics in political discourse. Her book; A Dirty War (2001) provided an unflinching look at the conflict's impact on ordinary people and solidified her reputation as a fearless journalist dedicated to exposing injustice.

Anna Politkovskaya's journalism significantly influenced public awareness regarding human rights abuses in Russia. Her reports brought attention to the suffering endured by civilians in Chechnya and challenged the Kremlin's narrative regarding its military operations. By shedding light on these issues, she played a crucial role in informing both domestic and international audiences about the realities of war. Politkovskaya authored several influential books that documented her experiences covering the Chechen conflict. Putin's Russia (2004) provided critical insights into Vladimir Putin's administration and its implications for civil liberties in Russia. Her writings received acclaim internationally; however, domestically they were met with hostility from government officials who viewed her as a threat. Her reports garnered numerous awards for their bravery and impact on journalism. Despite this recognition, Politkovskaya faced significant backlash for her outspoken criticism of Russian authorities. She was subjected to harassment, threats, and even physical violence as a result of her commitment to exposing human rights abuses.

On October 7th 2006, coincidentally Vladimir Putin's birthday, Anna Politkovskaya was assassinated in the elevator of her apartment building in Moscow. She had been shot multiple times at close range. The circumstances surrounding her murder raised suspicions that it was a contract killing orchestrated by those who sought to silence her voice. In the months leading up to her death, Politkovskaya had received numerous threats due to her reporting on sensitive topics related to government corruption and military actions in Chechnya. She had previously survived an assassination attempt when she was poisoned while traveling to negotiate during the Beslan school hostage crisis in 2004.

Imprisonment of Palestinian Minors

The recent passage of a law by the Israeli Knesset allowing the detention of Palestinian minors under the age of 14 marks a significant development in the ongoing Israeli-Palestinian conflict. This legislation, which permits courts to order the detention of children raises critical questions about the treatment of minors in conflict zones and the implications for human rights.

The Israeli-Palestinian conflict has deep historical roots, dating back to the early 20th century with the rise of nationalist movements. Tensions escalated with the establishment of Israel in 1948, leading to significant displacement and conflict. Over the decades, various wars and uprisings have shaped the dynamics between Israelis and Palestinians, with issues such as territory, sovereignty, and rights remaining contentious.

Historically, minors in conflict zones have been subject to various legal frameworks that often fail to protect their rights adequately. Internationally recognized norms, such as those outlined in the UN Convention on the Rights of the Child (CRC), emphasize the need for special protection for children. However, in practice, many countries including Israel have enacted laws that allow for the detention of minors under circumstances that contravene these international standards.

Israel justifies this new law on grounds of national security, asserting that it is necessary to combat terrorism effectively. The law allows for detention in closed facilities for children deemed dangerous or involved in serious offenses. Proponents argue that it is a measure aimed at deterring violence and protecting citizens. The law raises significant concerns when compared to international legal standards. The UN Convention on the Rights of the Child mandates that children should be treated with dignity and should not be deprived of liberty unlawfully or arbitrarily. Critics argue that Israel's legislation contravenes these principles by allowing for the detention of minors without adequate safeguards or due process.

The psychological impact on Palestinian minors subjected to detention can be profound. Research indicates that exposure to violence and incarceration can lead to long term mental health issues, including PTSD, anxiety, and depression. The trauma associated with detention, often involving isolation and harsh treatment can hinder emotional development and exacerbate existing vulnerabilities.

Testimonies from former detainees reveal harrowing experiences. For instance, accounts from children detail instances of physical abuse during detention and psychological manipulation aimed at extracting confessions under duress. Such narratives highlight the urgent need for reform in how minors are treated within the legal system.

Dahdouh Family Tragedy

On October 25th 2023, several family members of Wael Dahdouh, a prominent journalist with Al Jazeera, were killed in an Israeli airstrike at the Nuseirat Refugee Camp. The attack resulted in the deaths of his wife and three children, marking a devastating personal tragedy for Dahdouh and raising serious concerns about the safety of journalists and their families in conflict zones. Wael Dahdouh is a well-respected journalist known for his extensive coverage of the Israeli-Palestinian conflict. As a correspondent for Al Jazeera, he has reported on critical issues affecting Palestinians, providing insights into their struggles amid ongoing violence. His work has garnered international attention and highlighted the challenges faced by civilians in Gaza.

Eyewitnesses reported that the airstrike occurred while Dahdouh's family was at home. Local residents described hearing explosions followed by chaos as rescue workers rushed to the scene. Statements from fellow journalists expressed outrage over the targeting of Dahdouh's family, emphasizing that such actions create an atmosphere of fear among media personnel working in Gaza. The killing of Wael Dahdouh's family underscores the heightened risks faced by journalists operating in conflict areas like Gaza. Such incidents can lead to self-censorship among reporters who may hesitate to cover sensitive topics due to fears for their safety or that of their families. This reluctance can result in significant gaps in reporting on critical issues affecting civilians during conflicts. The tragedy also raises broader questions about press freedom in Palestine. When journalists are targeted or threatened, it undermines their ability to report freely and accurately. The chilling effect on journalism can lead to a lack of accountability for those committing human rights abuses during conflicts, ultimately harming public access to information.

Marielle Franco

Marielle Franco was a prominent Brazilian politician and human rights activist born on July 27th 1979, in Rio de Janeiro. She rose to prominence as a city councilor in Rio de Janeiro, where she became known for her outspoken criticism of police violence and systemic racism. Franco was a member of the Socialism and Liberty Party (PSOL) and was deeply committed to advocating for marginalized communities, particularly Afro-Brazilians.

On March 14th 2018 in Rio de Janeiro, Brazil Franco was shot dead in a targeted attack while returning home from an event promoting black women's empowerment. A car pulled alongside hers, and multiple shots were fired from inside the vehicle, killing her instantly. The assassination sparked national outrage and protests demanding justice for her murder and accountability for ongoing violence against women and minorities. Franco's death highlighted the severe risks faced by activists in Brazil who challenge entrenched power structures and advocate for human rights.

Brazil has a complex history regarding human rights issues, particularly concerning police violence against marginalized communities. The political environment at the time of Franco's activism was marked by increasing militarization of police forces and widespread allegations of abuse. According to Human Rights Watch (HRW), Brazil has one of the highest rates of police killings in the world. In 2020 alone, over 6,000 people were killed by police. The assassination of Marielle Franco is part of a broader pattern of violence against human rights defenders in Brazil. Since 1995, more than 1,000 human rights activists have been killed in the country. The conditions in Brazil created an environment hostile to activists like Franco, who faced significant risks for their work.

The impact of Marielle Franco's work and subsequent assassination reverberated throughout Brazilian society and politics. Her death galvanized public opinion against police violence and corruption. Following her murder, protests erupted across Brazil demanding justice for Franco and accountability for police violence. Her assassination became a rallying point for movements advocating for human rights. Various social movements emerged in response to her death, including campaigns focused on women's rights, racial equality, and police reform. Franco's legacy continues to inspire activism in Brazil as citizens demand greater accountability from their government.

In March 2024, Brazilian authorities arrested several individuals linked to her murder after years of investigation. These arrests included politicians allegedly involved in orchestrating the crime. An independent inquiry into Franco's murder has been called for by various organizations advocating for justice.

Boris Nemtsov

Boris Nemtsov was a prominent Russian politician born on October 9th 1959. He served as Deputy Prime Minister under President Boris Yeltsin and was widely regarded as a leading figure in the Russian opposition. Throughout his political career, Nemtsov was an outspoken critic of President Vladimir Putin and the corruption within his administration.

On February 27th 2015 in Moscow, Russia Nemtsov was shot dead near the Kremlin while walking with his girlfriend. At the time of his assassination, he was actively involved in organizing protests against Russia's military intervention in Ukraine and was preparing to release a report detailing evidence of Russian troops' involvement in Ukraine's conflict. His murder sparked widespread outrage both domestically and internationally, highlighting the risks faced by political dissidents in Russia. The assassination underscored the dangers associated with whistleblowing in an environment where dissent is often met with violence.

The political landscape in Russia has been characterized by increasing authoritarianism and systemic corruption since Vladimir Putin came to power. The environment for political dissidents has become increasingly hostile, with numerous activists facing harassment, imprisonment, or worse. According to Transparency International's Corruption Perceptions Index (CPI), Russia consistently ranks poorly regarding corruption. In 2021, it was ranked

136th out of 180 countries. The assassination of Boris Nemtsov is part of a broader pattern of violence against political activists in Russia. Since 2000, numerous journalists and opposition figures have been murdered under suspicious circumstances. These conditions create an environment where whistleblowers face significant risks for their work.

Santiago Maldonado

Santiago Maldonado was an Argentinian activist known for his support of indigenous rights, particularly those of the Mapuche community. His activism was rooted in a deep commitment to social justice and environmental protection, making him a significant figure in contemporary Argentine civil society. Maldonado's disappearance in August 2017 during a protest against police repression has since become emblematic of the struggles faced by activists in Argentina, highlighting issues of state violence and the need for accountability.

Leading up to Santiago Maldonado's disappearance, Argentina was grappling with significant challenges regarding indigenous rights. The Mapuche community had long been fighting for their ancestral land rights, particularly against the encroachment of large corporations like the Benetton Group. This struggle intensified as the government increasingly sided with corporate interests over indigenous claims.

On August 1st 2017, a peaceful protest was organized by the Mapuche community at Pu Lof de la Resistencia in Chubut Province to demand the release of their leader, Facundo Jones Huala, who was jailed under controversial circumstances. The protest escalated when the Argentine National Gendarmerie intervened violently to disperse demonstrators. Reports indicated that security forces used rubber bullets and live ammunition against protesters, leading to chaos and panic as individuals fled towards the

Chubut River. Santiago Maldonado was last seen during this violent police intervention on August 1st. Eyewitness accounts suggested he stayed behind to help others escape but subsequently disappeared amidst the turmoil. The immediate public response was one of outrage and concern, with widespread media coverage amplifying calls for justice and accountability. Activists and human rights organizations quickly labeled his disappearance as a potential enforced disappearance by state forces. As news of his disappearance spread, protests erupted across Argentina demanding answers from the government. The case drew international attention, prompting human rights organizations like Human Rights Watch to call for an independent investigation into Maldonado's fate.

The discovery of Santiago Maldonado's body on October 17th 2017, in the Chubut River brought both closure and further controversy. The official autopsy concluded that he died from drowning due to hypothermia, with no signs of violence on his body. However, many activists and family members rejected this conclusion, insisting that he was a victim of state violence.

Maldonado's case galvanized public awareness regarding police brutality against activists in Argentina. It served as a rallying point for indigenous rights movements and highlighted the ongoing struggles faced by marginalized communities in their fight for justice.

Ibrahim (A.S)

Abraham, known as Avraham in Hebrew and Ibrahim in Arabic, holds a pivotal role in the religious narratives of Judaism, Christianity, and Islam. He is often referred to as the "father of faith" due to his foundational status in these three major monotheistic religions. In Judaism, Abraham is celebrated as the patriarch who entered into a covenant with God, establishing the Israelites as His chosen people. In Christianity, he is viewed as a model of faith and righteousness, exemplifying the principle of salvation through belief. In Islam, Abraham is revered as a prophet and a Muslim, a term that denotes one who submits to God's will. The term Muslim derives from the Arabic root s-l-m, which means "to submit" or "to surrender." This concept is central to Islamic belief and practice, emphasizing obedience to God's commands. In the context of Abraham, this implies that he was one who submitted fully to God's will long before the advent of Islam as a formal religion.

Genesis 17:1 states;

"When Abram was ninety nine years old, the LORD appeared to Abram and said to him, 'I am God Almighty; walk before me and be blameless.'"

This verse marks a significant moment in the Abrahamic covenant, where God reaffirms His promises to Abraham. The phrase "walk before me and be blameless" signifies a call for Abraham to live righteously and faithfully in accordance with God's commands. The covenant established here is both a promise of descendants and land, emphasizing Abraham's role as a foundational figure for future generations.

The Targums are Aramaic translations and interpretations of the Hebrew Bible that reflect Jewish thought during the Second Temple period. Two notable Targums are Targum Onkelos and Targum Jonathan.

Targum Onkelos translates Genesis 17:1 similarly but emphasizes God's sovereignty by referring to Him as "the Lord God Almighty." The instruction for Abraham to be "blameless" is interpreted as an encouragement to maintain integrity in his relationship with God.

Targum Jonathan offers additional commentary by highlighting Abraham's faithfulness and commitment to God's commands. It may not explicitly use the term Muslim, but it aligns with the notion of submission to God's will.

Both Targums underscore Abraham's identity as a devoted servant of God, reflecting attributes that resonate with the Islamic understanding of being a Muslim; one who submits to divine authority.

The term 'Shelim' appears in some interpretations related to Genesis 17:1. Etymologically, it derives from the root meaning "whole" or "complete." This concept connects closely with being Muslim, as both terms embody notions of wholeness in faith and submission.

In Jewish thought, being tamim, translated here as "blameless," suggests an integrity that aligns with the Islamic ideal of submission. Thus, Abraham's character exemplifies these qualities, he is portrayed as a model believer whose life reflects complete devotion to God.

Abraham's portrayal in Jewish texts contrasts yet complements Islamic perspectives found in the Quran. In Islam, Ibrahim (A.S) is depicted as an archetype of monotheism who rejected polytheism long before Judaism or Christianity emerged. The Quran explicitly refers to him as a Muslim;

"When his Lord said to him, 'Submit!' he said, 'I have submitted to the Lord of the worlds.'" (Quran 2:131)

The narrative of Abraham's attempted sacrifice of his son is one of the most profound and debated stories in the Bible, primarily found in Genesis 22.

Genesis 22;

Sometime later God tested Abraham. He said to him, "Abraham!" "Here I am," he replied.

Then God said, "Take your son, ***your only son***, whom you love, Isaac, and go to the region of Moriah. Sacrifice him there as a burnt offering on a mountain I will show you."

Since Ishmael PBUH was the first born son; the deduction is that he was ***the only son*** at that time i.e. it was before Isaac PBUH was born proving that this verse was corrupted by switching the names of the two sons.

Traditionally, it is believed that Isaac was the intended sacrifice. However Ishmael PBUH, Abraham's firstborn son, was the intended victim. This perspective not only challenges conventional interpretations within Judaism and Christianity but also aligns with Islamic traditions that recognize Ishmael PBUH as the sacrificial figure.

Zephaniah 3:9

The Book of Zephaniah, a text from the Hebrew Bible, addresses themes of judgment and restoration during a tumultuous period in ancient Judah, particularly under King Josiah's reign (640-609 BCE). Zephaniah 3:9 states, "For then will I turn to the people a pure language that they may all call upon the name of the LORD, to serve him with one consent" (KJV). This verse is pivotal as it speaks to the restoration of worship and unity among the people.

The verse Zephaniah 3:9 appears in two prominent translations:

King James Version (KJV): "For then will I turn to the people a pure language that they may all call upon the name of the LORD, to serve him with one consent."

New International Version (NIV): "Then I will purify the lips of the peoples, that all of them may call on the name of the LORD and serve him shoulder to shoulder."

Key terms and phrases include "pure language" (KJV) and "purify the lips" (NIV), both suggesting a transformation leading to unified worship. The phrase "shoulder to shoulder" in NIV evokes imagery of communal prayer, resonating with Islamic practices where worshippers stand closely together during prayers.

Islamic communal prayer is characterized by several key features:

*Shoulder to Shoulder Formation; Worshippers line up closely during prayers, symbolizing unity.

*Use of Arabic; Arabic serves as the lingua franca in Islamic worship, fostering a shared linguistic identity among diverse Muslim communities.

WhatsApp

YouTube

Telegram

The white liberal differs from the white conservative only in one way; the liberal is more deceitful than the conservative.

El-Hajj Malik El-Shabazz

www.ingramcontent.com/pod-product-compliance
Lightning Source LLC
LaVergne TN
LVHW041023150826
845672LV00001B/182